PROPHETS
THE VOICES OF YAHWEH

PROPHETS
THE VOICES OF YAHWEH

G. STEVE KINNARD

DPI
DISCIPLESHIP
PUBLICATIONS
INTERNATIONAL

Prophets

© 2001 by Discipleship Publications International
2 Sterling Road, Billerica, Mass. 01862-2595

Printed in the United States of America

ISBN 1-57782-169-6

Cover & Interior Design: Tony Bonazzi

CONTENTS

ACKNOWLEDGMENTS

I would like to warmly thank all those who helped me to see this project to completion. Thanks...

...to Leigh, my wife, for all her love and support through the years. I dedicate this book to you.

...to Chelsea and Daniel, my daughter and son, who allowed me to type, type, type when they wanted to play, play, play.

...to Joan Perryman, for editing the text and making it readable. Joan, I owe you a great debt.

...to the staff of Discipleship Publications International for taking on this project and seeing it through to completion. You are an amazing group. Thanks for all that you do for the kingdom of God.

...to Thomas Oh, who checked the scripture references.

...to Rupert and Lisa Burtan, for proofing the notes.

...to Cassandra Conyers, for her encouragement and help.

...to Steve and Lisa Johnson, lifelong friends, who encouraged me along the way.

...to Randy Tinnen, Geoffery Owens and Chris Broom, who helped with specific chapters.

...to John and Vivian Hanes for computer assistance and for their friendship and constant encouragement.

...to Todd Wilson, for more computer assistance.

...to Larry Salburg, for his help with editing—and his friendship and support.

...to Corrin Oh, for saving me from hours in front of the computer.

...to Art Shirley and his daughter, Ann, who scanned the four-hundred-page manuscript into Word format. (I originally wrote this book by using a typewriter before I knew how to use a computer!)

...to the members and staff of the New York City Church of Christ, who allowed me to talk about the same subject for more than five years as I completed this work.

PART I

INTRODUCTION

INTRODUCTION

It is a foolish thing to make a long prologue and to be short in the story itself.

2 Maccabees 2:32

This book has been a labor of love. It represents more than thirteen years of my life—five years of study and research to write it and another eight to publish it. During those years I have been drawn closer to God through the vision of the prophets. The prophets understood the nature of God. As they saw God's glory, he changed them. He took ordinary men and women and gave them an extraordinary message. They passionately proclaimed this message to their world. As we begin to understand the message God gave to the prophets, we will be changed.

My study of the prophets has helped me to become more of a prophet. Their character is contagious. They were bold, spiritual, devoted, radical and peculiar. They broke social norms and set traditions aside. They ventured into deep waters, exploring the truth about God, religion, humanity and sin. They preached the great themes of God—love, grace, hope, peace and salvation. The more you study the prophets, the more they influence you. You begin to become like them.

As a Christian writer, I believe that everything ultimately points to and is concerned with the center of reality—Jesus Christ of Nazareth. The prophets looked forward to the coming Messiah. As they looked forward to his coming, God revealed himself to them in their day and time. Although the prophets did not have the full picture of God as revealed through Jesus, I hope that we can still appreciate the mystical and miraculous manner in which God worked in the lives of the prophets of Israel.

What separates this book from other introductions to the prophetic literature? Some introductions delve into the critical questions concerning the prophets and miss the practical beauty of the prophetic message. Other books emphasize the message of the prophets but neglect the critical questions that must be asked. This book attempts to blend the critical and the practical. Very few commentaries or critical introductions do this. My aim is to both answer the critical questions that confront each prophetic text and to consider the powerful, practical message of each prophet of Israel.

David Rosenberg, author of a great translation of the Old Testament—*A Poet's Bible*—wrote:

> The Bible, arguably the most important work of art in the Western literary canon, is an uneasy subject in the classroom. Why are our great poetic stories taught in the dullest of ways? I believe the fault can be traced to a failure of imagination in academic life. Imagination can be stifled by dogma, but it can also be flattened by theories that handle merely the skeletons of texts. The Bible is a luminous guidebook to our past yet it is put out of reach by colorless professors. And the broad range of poets who gave voice to the original words have been rendered voiceless by prosaic translations. Once, the poets lent us what one critic has called, in the context of soul music, the "spiritual magnitude of the individual voice." It is time to rediscover the original text.[1]

In his translation, Rosenberg rediscovers the text by capturing the poetic beauty of the Hebrew language. My hope for Prophets is that it will help the Bible student to "rediscover the text."

This book is divided into two sections, to be covered in three separate volumes. The first section, the present volume, introduces the prophetic material to the reader. In chapter 1 we embark on our journey, asking three important questions along the way: Who is God? Who are the prophets? And who are we? In chapter 2 we define the term "prophecy." Chapter 3 identifies the character of a prophet. Chapters 4–11 are historical surveys to be used for reference, as one would use a Bible dictionary. Chapters 4–8 present an overview of the many people in the Bible who were prophets; chapters 9–11 form a historical survey of the kings of Israel, from the reign of Solomon to the close of the Old Testament.

---

[1] David Rosenberg, *A Poet's Bible* (New York: Hyperion, 1991) xi.

The next section, contained in volumes two and three, begins with the book of Amos, the first of the written prophets. A critical introduction is given of every prophet of the Old Testament in chronological order. These introductions do not serve as substitutes for reading the Biblical text, but as helps for understanding the text. Read these introductions as you read the corresponding books in your Bible.

For each prophet, material is given to clarify what occurs in the Biblical text. The material is presented in an order that begins with an overview, moves to more detailed information and closes with a practical lesson. Each chapter is divided as follows:

1. Date
2. Location
3. Purpose
4. Theme
5. Meaning of Name
6. Audience
7. Outline
8. Memory Work
9. Special Notes
10. Historical Context
11. The Person
12. The Call
13. Structure and Form
14. Theology
15. Messianic Expectation
16. Important Passage
17. Bibliography

Throughout the book, I refer to the God of Israel by using the name, "Yahweh." I prefer it to "Jehovah," and believe this name comes much closer to the pronunciation of the name revealed to Moses on Sinai.

I used a number of different Bible translations in this work. My primary translation is the *Revised Standard Version*. Unless noted in the text, this is the translation used. Other translations are used as well, and their abbreviations are listed as follows:

NEB—*The New English Bible*
NIV—*New International Version*
JB—*The Jerusalem Bible*
Tanakh—*Tanakh—The Holy Scriptures: The New Jewish Publication Society Translation According to the Traditional Hebrew Text*
PB—*A Poet's Bible*

Finally, let me say a word about an unconventional feature of these volumes. I have chosen to include several fictional accounts of the lives of my heroes, the great prophets of Israel. I am aware that certain modern elements have been transported into these ancient settings, and that I have on occasion taken liberties with the silence of the Biblical record. As popular theologian and author Calvin Miller once quipped, "Creativity can be a curse. Ask Dr. Frankenstein." I had a lot of fun with these fictional pieces, but my primary purpose for interjecting them into this work is to help us get the "flavor" of the prophets in a "right-brain" sort of way. Hopefully these musings will draw you further into the real-life drama of the prophets and allow you to better understand the spirit of these powerful men and women of God as they really were.

Now awaits the study of the prophets. This is a study that may begin with this book, but it will not end here. In the words of John Fitzgerald Kennedy:

> All this will not be finished in the first one hundred days. Nor will it be finished in the first one thousand days, nor even perhaps in our lifetime on this planet. But let us begin.

Let us begin.

G. S. K.
November 1993
Updated August 2001

AN AFTERNOON TALK

My thoughts and feelings seem to be getting more and more like those of the Old Testament, and in recent months I have been reading the Old Testament much more than the New. It is only when one knows the unutterability of the name of God that one can utter the name of Jesus Christ; it is only when one loves life and the earth so much that without them everything seems to be over, that one can believe in the resurrection and a new world; it is only when one submits to God's law that one can speak of grace; and it is only when God's wrath and vengeance are hanging as grim realities over the heads of one's enemies that something of what it means to love and forgive them can touch our hearts.

—Dietrich Bonhoeffer
a letter written from a Nazi prison
a Sunday in 1943

I was just twelve when my grandfather died. Now I'm thirty-eight and have children of my own. I still remember Granddad as if I had just seen him yesterday. My last meeting with him is deeply etched in my mind.

Granddad seemed to be eternally old—so old you could smell the dust on his breath when he talked. The lines on his face were like gullies. He was majestic, yet plain; regal, yet common. His robe was simple, without design. His ruddy staff, which he leaned on even when he sat, was made from a beautiful red cedar from Lebanon. His beard was as gray as the sky over the Sea of Galilee just before an afternoon thunderstorm. His voice was low and raspy and was a voice of experience. It was as if you could hear all of our ancestors speaking through him. At twelve, I was intimidated by him. Yet, strangely enough, I considered him a friend.

You can imagine my mixed emotions when, on a clear afternoon in April, I received word that my grandfather wanted to see me. I was getting ready for a big ball game with my friends down the street when I received his message. I was nervous. It was not the ridicule of my friends that bothered me—I could handle that—but he had never sent for me before—not like this, out of the blue, without warning.

I remember the feeling I had when I turned down his street and faced his door. My stomach almost leaped out of my mouth. My heart pounded like a drum. I wiped the sweat off the palm of my right hand and then formed a fist and rapped on his door. There was no answer. I was relieved. Maybe he was not at home. When I turned to leave, the wind blew the door ajar. I stepped inside and sheepishly said, "Granddad?"

From a dark corner of the small, ancient room came a low, sleepy voice, "Yes, yes, who is it? And why are you waking me from my sleep?"

"You sent for me, didn't you?"

"Oh yes, that's right. I just didn't expect you to come during my nap."

"I'm sorry, Granddad. It's just as well, really, because I have a big ball game today. I'll just come back later."

"No, no, Son. I'm awake now. Come on in. Let's talk."

"But, Granddad, what about the game? Josh and Gabe are waiting for me at the field."

"They will just have to play for a while without you. We need to talk."

"Can't we just talk tonight?"

"Tonight is the Sabbath, Son. We will be busy with our Sabbath obligations.

"Okay. But can we make it quick?"

"Quick! Quick? You know that 'quick' and me are best friends."

Granddad was hard of hearing, so I said under my breath, "I never knew that you and 'quick' had even met."

"What's that, Son?" he asked.

"Nothing, Gramps. Nothing."

Grandfather used his cedar staff to push himself up from his cot, and then he sat down in a chair next to a cluttered table. He said, "Our lesson today is on the prophets. Do you know who the prophets were?"

I answered, "Sure. Isaiah, Jeremiah, Ezekiel and Daniel."

"That's right, but there were many other prophets as well. In fact, anyone who was God's spokesman was a prophet."

"So Moses was a prophet?"

"That's right, Son. He was the prophet *par excellence*."

"What does that mean?"

"It means that he was the best."

Once again, under my breath, I muttered, "Why didn't you just say so?"

"What's that?"

"Nothing."

"'Nothing,' again. If you want me to go quickly, why waste time with 'nothings'?"

"Sorry, Granddad."

"That's okay. Let's continue. Who would you consider to be the most powerful prophet to have ever lived?"

"I have no idea."

"Would you guess Elijah?"

"Elijah sounds good to me," I replied.

"Why don't I tell you all I know about Elijah?"

"Please, Granddad! Remember the game."

"Okay, then. Why don't I tell you a few interesting stories about the prophets? Maybe then you could still make your game."

"That sounds great!" I said joyfully.

My grandfather was in his element when he talked about the prophets. They were his passion. Whenever he talked about them, his face would brighten and his expression would intensify. He knew as much as any man I've ever met about the prophets of Israel. Rabbis came to him for insight about the prophetic messengers.

He began, "Elijah was a wild man. He stood against one of the most wicked kings of the northern kingdom of Israel, King Ahab. He was the thorn in Ahab's side. Anywhere Ahab turned, Elijah was there to face him down. Once, on Mount Carmel, Elijah challenged all the prophets of Baal to a duel—his God against their gods."

"Who won?"

"What kind of a question is that? 'Who won?' Who do you think won?!"

"Calm down, Granddad. I was only joking."

"May I continue?"

"Yes, please."

He continued as if he had not missed a beat. "After experiencing that powerful victory over the prophets of Baal, guess what Elijah did next?"

"What?"

"He ran away from a woman named Jezebel, Ahab's wife."

The thought of a prophet running from a woman made me angry.

"No way," I said. "And this is your 'most powerful prophet of all time'? Was he a man or a woman? I would never run from a woman."

I could tell this did not sit well with my grandfather. He used his staff to lift himself from his chair, and he hobbled behind me. I was afraid to look around and face him. I sat frozen in my chair, staring straight at the wall ahead of me.

During this time, he kept talking, "Yes, he was a prophet, but he was human. He gave in to fear just like you or me. Jezebel was powerful. She put Elijah's face on all the 'wanted' posters around town, and Elijah felt alone. He ran out of town like a puppy that has been beaten, and he found himself hiding from Jezebel on a mountain in the wilderness. Who do you think showed up to have a little talk with Elijah on that mountain?"

I answered, "I give up. Who?"

But no answer came. I turned around, and my Grandfather had vanished. I gingerly rose from my chair and started toward the dark corner of the room. I whispered, "Granddad?" No answer. I tried again, "Granddad?" There was still no answer. I tried again, "This is not funny, Granddad. Where are you?"

Then, from out of the dark came rushing a wild, maniacal half-human, half-monster sort of thing with a huge log in its arm, screaming Philistine curses at the top of its lungs. I jumped back across the room, grabbed the chair and held it in front of me, hoping to fend off this monstrous beast.

"Stay back!" I screamed.

Then I heard a low thunder of laughter from the dark corner I had vacated. I knew I had been fooled. As he talked, Grandfather had taken some makeup and transformed himself into "the beast of the dark corner."

Once he had controlled his laughter, he said, "So, you wouldn't be afraid of a woman, right? You almost jumped out of your skin at the game of an old man."

By this time I was angry, "Stop playing games!" I said. "If I wanted to play games, I would be with Josh and Gabe right now."

He taunted me, "But I didn't think I could scare you. You're a man, not a woman."

"That was not fair," I grumbled.

At this point I expected an apology. Instead I received a serious, "Life seldom is." Then, as he took off his makeup, he went on.

"Anyway, who was on the mountain with Elijah? God was. Lightning flashed, the thunder roared, and a mighty wind almost blew Elijah off his feet. After this great light show came a silence so intense it was eerie. It was a silence so still and foreboding that Elijah, with ears of faith, knew that God was speaking in the silence. Elijah heard God whisper, 'Why are you up here on this mountain when there are seven thousand others just like you still doing their jobs in Samaria without bowing a knee to Baal?' I am sure that Elijah must have been embarrassed to think that he was afraid of a mean woman while all the time God was on his side. The lesson here is that greatness is not always measured by your victories, but by how you handle your defeats."

I added, "That is a lesson I hope I never have to learn."

Granddad replied, "You will, Son. Believe me, you will."

"Now let me tell you about the written prophets," Granddad said.

"The written prophets?" I asked.

"Yes, these were the prophets who left behind a written record of their lives."

"Like Jeremiah?"

"Jeremiah, that's right. But first there was Amos."

"Who was Amos?" I asked.

He answered, "Amos was a shepherd from Tekoa and a sycamore-fig tree keeper."

"You're kidding? I thought only great and powerful men could be prophets."

"No, Son. The prophets were often unassuming, ordinary men and women. They were no different from you or me. It was the Lord who made them extraordinary."

"What is 'extra...ordinary'?" I asked. "Does that mean 'incredibly ordinary'? Much more ordinary than anyone else, like dull Barnabas, down at the bakery?"

"No, Son. It means that he was special. He was out of the ordinary. He was not your average Adam."

"What was extraordinary about Amos?"

Once again, Granddad got that look in his eye, which he only got when he talked about the prophets. He said, "Amos was the only prophet from the southern kingdom of Judah to trek northward into Samaria and challenge the nation of Israel. He had the eyes of a prophet. He saw what everyone else missed. He noticed the fat women sitting on their ivory couches sipping fine wine from the vineyards of Mount Hermon while their slave boys fanned them with fans made of peacock feathers. He noticed the rich landowner who seemed blind when stepping over the homeless in the street but who would spot the dirt left in a migrant worker's hair and, with the arrogance of Caesar, would have the poor man place the clod of mud back in his field. Amos walked into Samaria like a gunslinger looking for a fight. He stopped the conversation at the bars during happy hour to tell society's elite that there were going to be consequences for their treatment of the poor."

Then my grandfather began building something out of small things scattered across his room. He piled pots upon scrolls and sandals on pots, and pillows upon sandals. As he talked, I discovered that he was building an altar—an altar like the one in Bethel. He said, "You think a prophet should have guts. Right,

Son? Well, let me tell you, Amos had guts. He had conviction—a deep conviction that God was on his side. He marched right into the sanctuary of Bethel on one of the high holy days and struck the altar of Israel with his staff to symbolize what God was going to do to Samaria. He struck that altar and smashed it all to pieces."

As he spoke, he took his cedar staff and swung it as if he was looking at the face of the devil himself in that pile of junk on his floor. Pots exploded, scrolls were ripped, feathers flew from the pillows, and a sandal shot across the floor and hit me in the face, cutting the corner of my lip. He swung until nothing was left in that little space of floor that had once held his crudely built altar. And when nothing was left, he swung once more to erase any memory of an altar that might still have been lurking about.

I stood dumbfounded. I did not know if I was more amazed at Amos or my grandfather. I could think of nothing to say.

Noting my silence, he continued, "After this great symbolic act, he slipped back into Judah, never to be heard from again."

"Never?" I asked.

"Not ever."

He paused. It was as if he was savoring the story, allowing it to set in. After a few moments he asked, "Should I go on?"

I looked at my ball and then glanced at the sunlight pouring through the window. The truth was, I had gotten so caught up in the story that I had no idea how much time had passed in his telling it. But I did not want my granddad to know the truth. I shrugged my shoulders, and in my most indifferent voice said, "I guess you can go ahead."

He asked, "You're sure? I wouldn't want to keep you from your game."

"Yes," I said, "just hurry."

"Let me tell you about Hosea," Granddad continued.

"Gomer's husband," I added.

"Yes," he said in amazement. "How did you know that?"

"How could you forget a name like 'Gomer'?"

"Of course. Hosea demonstrated how far God will go to teach love to his prophets. Have you ever loved someone who did not love you back?"

"Please, Gramps. I'm only twelve."

"Right. Well, God wanted Hosea to know what it felt like to love someone who did not love him back. This would deepen Hosea's understanding of God. So he asked Hosea to marry a prostitute."

Not wanting my granddad to know that I understood what prostitutes were, I asked, "What's a prostitute?"

My grandfather stuttered, "Oh boy, how do I explain this one? Okay. Well, you know how much I love your Grandma, right?"

"Yes."

"Well, what would you think if you saw your Grandma kissing another man?"

"I'd be sick."

"What if she kissed any man who would give her a new bracelet, or a new ring, or a few pieces of gold?"

To save him further embarrassment, I said, "I get the picture, Granddad."

He asked, "If she behaved that way, would you think that I should leave her?"

"It is difficult to imagine," I replied. "But, yes, I would think so."

"Well, that's how Hosea's wife acted, but God told Hosea to stay with her. Hosea would go off to preach, and when he came back, Gomer was nowhere to be found. She would sell herself on a street corner or would dance in front of strangers. When she had children, they bore no resemblance to Hosea. Once, after he had been away preaching, his neighbors told him that Gomer had shacked up in a dirty room above a winery. She had been there for a couple of months. She had lost her front teeth in a fight and had some horrible scars from rough treatment. But Hosea scraped together everything he had to buy out her contract and take her back home."

"Why would God ask Hosea to keep living with her?" I asked.

"Why? Because God had been living with Israel for centuries, buying her back after her adulteries and loving her as a new bride. God did not ask Hosea to do anything that he himself had not already done. Hosea learned what 'God is love' really means."

"It still seems severe," I added.

"It was severe; but God wanted Hosea to understand, firsthand, what God experienced with Israel. To be a prophet was not a glorious task. It was often humbling and grueling. Each prophet experienced God in a unique way. Hosea married a prostitute, but Isaiah had a wife who shared the ministry of prophecy with him. Speaking of Isaiah, what do you know of him?"

"Isaiah? Granddad, why ask me? You are the expert."

"Tell me what you know about him," he shot back.

"At school, they say his book was written by three different people," I replied.

"They do, do they?"

"Yes," I continued, "and they are not sure if Isaiah had much to do with the book of Isaiah at all."

At this point my grandfather's face became flushed. Through clenched teeth he said, "They are fools."

"Fools, Gramps? They are my teachers."

"Fools—bigheaded, overeducated fools! They limit the power of God! Why is it so hard to believe that God could use one man to write the text of Isaiah? Why is it so hard to accept that God could predict, centuries before it happened, the destruction of Jerusalem and the return of the exiles? If God wanted to name Cyrus, king of the Persians, by name, decades before he was born, couldn't he do so? Of course he could. Those fools limit the power of God. They do not believe that God works supernaturally. Therefore, they pick apart the book of Isaiah."

I stepped in. "Calm down, Granddad. I said that they teach that garbage; I did not say that I believe it."

"Well, you shouldn't; they're fools. What do they really know of Isaiah?!"

Then my grandfather slipped into that look, his mystical look, as if he were looking at God himself. He continued, "Isaiah was the diamond of the Old Testament prophets. He saw what others only dream of. He saw the Mystery: the One who was, and is, and is to come. He saw him as a thousand lights flickering off and on, and on and off. He saw him as angels who flew back and forth, and forth and back, all the while saying, "Holy, holy, holy—holy, holy, holy." As he stood before the Mystery, he gasped for air. As the wind left his lungs, he fell forward on his knees, not knowing whether to hide or to run. He did not know what to say—he was so frozen with awe. He found himself confessing, 'I am a sorry dog. A man with unclean lips.' And the Mystery approached him and with a burning coal, touched Isaiah's lips. Isaiah screamed in pain, and as the pain left, he asked, 'What? What must I do now?' The Mystery answered back, 'Go!' And Isaiah asked, 'Where?' The Mystery said, 'To the ends of the earth and back. From the first newborn child to the last dying old man. Go from here to there and back again.' Then Isaiah, with his charred lips, asked, 'How long?' And the Mystery answered, 'Till hell freezes over. Till all is over and done.' And Isaiah went. He started when he heard the call, and he did not stop until he drew his last breath."

Once again, I was speechless. I heard in my grandfather's voice the passion of Isaiah.

He continued, "Isaiah was the diamond. But after the diamond came a time of silence. Decade after decade slipped by, and the voice of God was not heard."

"Why not?" I inquired.

"No one knows," he replied. "Maybe God felt that he had sent enough messengers for that generation, and he needed a whole new generation to come along who would listen to his voice."

"Then came Jeremiah, the weeping prophet."

"Why did he weep?"

"He wept for the people of Judah who had calloused their hearts to the point of not responding to God's call. Jeremiah was in the prophetic ministry for more than four decades. He saw five kings of Judah come and go. He also saw Jerusalem's freedom disappear, as the Babylonians swept into Judah and took the land by storm. Jeremiah might have been the loneliest prophet to have ever lived. It seems everyone wanted to kill him. But you must realize, Jeremiah brought it on himself. He preached a message of doom. He put down everything that was happening in Judah. He lambasted the king and the priests. He preached against idols and extramarital sex. He spoke out against the rich, who abused the poor. The politicians, clergy members and the rich were only going to take this for so long.

"One king with whom Jeremiah had a dispute was Zedekiah of Judah. After their disagreement, Zedekiah did what any other egomaniacal king in his position would have done—he ordered for Jeremiah to be killed. The princes threw Jeremiah in the cistern of Malchi'ah and left him for dead. The cistern was low on water, so Jeremiah sunk up to his armpits in the muck.

"An Ethiopian eunuch who was in the king's court heard of the incident and said to the king, 'Zedekiah, you know you have thrown God's man in a cistern. He will die of hunger in that cistern if you do not do something. How do you think God will take to you killing one of his prophets like this?' Zedekiah listened to the foreigner, and he allowed the Ethiopian to take thirty men with him to pull Jeremiah out. They tied together old rags and pulled and pulled until they saw a figure resembling a mud pie reaching for the top of the well.

"Jeremiah could have called it quits at this point. This was not the first time he had come within a breath of his life for preaching the truth. The fact is that Jeremiah could not stop preaching—it would have killed him. The moment he stopped preaching, he would have shriveled up and died. The word of God was like a fire in his bones, and he could not help but speak. He was going to suffer for the things he said. But it would have hurt him much more to have said nothing."

I said, "I would have called it quits."

I could tell that Grandfather was a bit upset at my saying this. He responded, "I know your heart, Son. If God called you to do something for him, be it great or small, you would do it and do it willingly."

What could I say? Perhaps he did know my heart. I have thought about it many times since that day. God did ask me to do some peculiar acts for him. And I did them, willingly. I believe that Grandfather not only knew my heart, but he prepared my heart. In some way he sensed certain things that were to come.

My grandfather asked, "Did you know that your brother was named after one of the prophets?"

"No, but I don't think I'll like this prophet—especially if he is anything like my brother."

"Oh, I think you will. Ezekiel was wild, gutsy and radical—a man's man—absolutely nothing like your weak brother. Ezekiel was a prophet of the exile."

I asked, "What was the exile?"

Grandfather explained, "The exile was the time when the children of Israel were taken into captivity in Babylon. They stayed there for five decades until Cyrus of Persia released them. Many people in exile thought Ezekiel was crazy. He did outlandish acts to demonstrate his prophecies. Once, he built a model of Jerusalem in the streets of Babylon, and he lay down in front of it to symbolize the siege of Jerusalem."

I interjected, "That doesn't sound so strange."

He responded, "That is not the whole story. He lay down on one side for 390 days—that's a year and a month, you know. Then he turned over and lay down on the other side for forty more days. Imagine spending more than a year of your life doing that."

"That's unbelievable."

"Unbelievable, but true."

It was happening again. My grandfather had that mystical look in his eye. He was transfixed by the message. He pulled out a sword that he had used in the army as a young man. I knew that the sword existed, but I had never actually seen it. It was beautiful. He handled it with care and ease, shifting it from one hand to the other. He felt its weight, reminding himself of its balance. With the sword in his right hand, he reached up with his left and grabbed a handful of his own hair. With the quickness of a cat, he cut a handful of hair off his gray head and dangled it before me. Then he continued with the story, demonstrating step by step as he went.

"And that's not all that Ezekiel did. He took his sword and shaved his head with it. He must have been a strange sight, with nicks and cuts all over his bald head. He picked his hair up from the ground and threw some of it in a fire. He cut some with the sword, threw some to the wind, and placed some in his belt—later taking some from the belt and throwing it in the fire. Hair went flying everywhere. This symbolized how Judah would be decimated by the Babylonians."

I was now transfixed. I was developing a greater appreciation for my grandfather. The way he handled the sword amazed me, but it was the way he told the stories that earned my respect. And now, with sword in hand, he began a dance. He kicked his chair toward the wall, pushed the table away and cleared the floor. As if on cue, I jumped back to a safe corner to watch. He swung the sword from side to side, from one hand to another, leaping and shouting in an ancient dialect. At times it seemed he became young again, jumping higher than any eighty-year-plus man was supposed to. Then he sang a song as he danced. Months later I found the song in the book of Ezekiel. He sang, acting each verse as he went:

> And the word of the LORD came to me: "Son of man, prophesy and say, Thus says the LORD, Say:
>
> A sword, a sword is sharpened
>   and also polished,
> sharpened for slaughter,
>   polished to flash like lightning!
>
> Or do we make mirth? You have despised the rod, my son, with everything of wood. So the sword is given to be polished, that it may be handled; it is sharpened and polished to be given into the hand of the slayer. Cry and wail, son of man, for it is against my people; it

> is against all the princes of Israel; they are delivered
> over to the sword with my people. Smite therefore upon
> your thigh. For it will not be a testing—what could it do if
> you despise the rod?" says the Lord GOD.
>
> "Prophesy therefore, son of man; clap your hands
> and let the sword come down twice, yea thrice, the sword
> for those to be slain; it is the sword for the great slaughter,
> which encompasses them, that their hearts may melt, and
> many fall at all their gates. I have given the glittering
> sword; ah! it is made like lightning, it is polished for slaugh-
> ter. Cut sharply to right and left where your edge is direct-
> ed. I also will clap my hands, and I will satisfy my fury; I
> the Lord have spoken." (Ezekiel 21:8-17)

When he finished singing, he stared up at the ceiling for a few moments and then looked at me in the corner of the room. He walked toward me. He lifted the sword above his head and made mighty circles with it. Just as he reached me, he fell to his knees and placed the sword at my feet. "I want you to have this," was all he said.

I was in shock. I dropped the ball I had been clutching in my hands all afternoon, and it went bouncing across the room. I bent over and picked up the sword. It was heavy—and wet with my grandfather's sweat. I still have the sword. I never learned to use it like my grandfather, but I cherish the gift. I looked at my grandfather as I had never looked at him before. My mouth said, "Thanks"—pure and simple. But he looked at my eyes. With my eyes, I said, "I love you, Granddad. I have never appreciated you like I should have, and for that I'm sorry. But I want you to know that from now and evermore, I love you with the deepest love I have ever felt for any person." He understood. It was the unsaid that meant everything to Granddad.

He looked back at me. With his mouth, he said, "You're welcome." But with his eyes, he said, "You're special. God has great plans for you. All the things I've dreamed of doing, you are going to do. God has chosen you. Prepare yourself for his call." I thought of dozens of questions that I wanted to ask. But I knew I would get no answer from him that day. Time would answer all my questions.

"Well, that's all for today. Go along and play." His voice broke the silence.

"We can't end here." I interjected, "Isn't there more? How about Haggai or Habakkuk, Daniel or Jonah?"

"I'm sorry. I've used up your whole afternoon," he said. "You missed your ball game, and you've had to listen to me rattle on for hours. We're done—you can go home."

I looked at him and said, "It's okay, Granddad. I really don't mind. The Sabbath will begin in a few minutes. Isn't there more? I really would like to hear more."

"You're sure?"

"Yes, I'm sure."

"I would like to tell you about the Prophet who is still to come."

"Still to come?"

"Yes. He is the Prophet about whom all the prophets spoke. He is the King of kings, the Son of David who will sit upon the throne of David and rule the nations. You need to know about him, and you need to anticipate his coming. After all, you are in the lineage of David yourself. Perhaps the Prophet of prophets will be your son."

"My son? No way, Granddad," I announced. "Don't talk like that. I'm not a king. You're a carpenter; my father is a carpenter; I'm going to be a carpenter; and my son is destined to be the son of a carpenter. Besides, Granddad, could anything good ever come out of Nazareth?"

"You never know, child. After all, wasn't David just a shepherd before he was king? Son, stay righteous, study, love the Torah and obey it—the Prophet of prophets just might be the son of a carpenter."

Just before I left my grandfather's house that day, he wrapped his sword in an old sheepskin and tied it up with twine. He asked me not to unwrap it until my thirtieth birthday—the year I would be fully recognized as an adult according to our tradition. I respected his request, and late in the evening on that special day, I pulled out the sheepskin and unwrapped the sword. It looked just as bright as the day he gave it to me. It had not tarnished, even slightly. As I picked it up and held it in my hand, the words of my grandfather came back to me—the words he had said with his eyes, not his lips: "All the things I've dreamed of doing, you are going to do. God has chosen you. Prepare yourself for his call."

I was twelve when I last saw Grandfather. Today my firstborn turned twelve. My wife, Mary, and I took him to Jerusalem with us. He became separated from us, and we frantically searched the city for him. We decided to go to the temple to pray that God would lead us to him. And that is where we found him, sitting and talking to some gray-headed elders. As I drew near, I was astonished to hear him speaking about Isaiah and Jeremiah with the same intensity and passion that my grandfather had shown years before. Only this time, it was the elders who sat in amazement.

PROPHETIC LITERACY TEST

Before you continue in this book, first take this prophetic literacy test. After you have finished your study of the prophets, take the test again and compare your results.

1. Who was the first person in the Bible to be given the designation of "prophet"?
2. Which prophet spoke to a donkey?
3. Which prophet was paid a quarter of a shekel of silver for locating lost donkeys?
4. Which court prophet rebuked David for his sin with Bathsheba?
5. Who prophesied to Jeroboam that he would lead the ten tribes of Israel?
6. Which prophet destroyed two troops of soldiers with fire when they attempted to arrest him?
7. Who is mentioned as being bald?
8. Which king is mentioned alongside a parading group of musical prophets?
9. Name three of the four prophetesses mentioned in the Old Testament.
10. Who was the only prophet from Judah to prophesy to Israel?
11. Which prophet was told to marry a prostitute?
12. Which prophet of the exile interpreted the dreams of Nebuchadnezzar?
13. Who comforted Judah by prophesying the coming doom of Nineveh?
14. Who was traditionally portrayed as a man with a lamp, searching the streets of Jerusalem for a sinner to punish?
15. Which prophet was a partner in his prophetic ministry with his wife?
16. Which prophet outran a chariot?
17. Which prophet rebuked David for taking a census?
18. Which prophet ran around stripped and barefoot for three years?
19. Which prophet was in all likelihood a eunuch?

20. Which prophet of the exile was not allowed to mourn for his wife when she died?
21. According to tradition, who prophesied when he was eighty years old?
22. Which prophet sunk up to his armpits in mud after being thrown into a cistern?
23. Which prophet asked, "Will a man rob God?" (NIV).
24. Which prophet stated that all Yahweh requires of his followers is to act justly, love mercy and walk humbly?
25. Which prophet of the exile shaved his head with a sword?
26. Which philosopher prophet said, "The righteous will live by his faith"? (NIV)
27. Who was the weeping prophet?
28. Who predicted that a severe locust plague would overtake Judah?
29. Who was the first woman in the Bible to be mentioned as a prophetess?
30. Which prophetess was also a judge of Israel?
31. Which prophet was the first to be associated with a group or school of prophets?
32. Who is distinguished as David's court prophet and seer?
33. Who hid one hundred prophets in two caves from King Ahab?
34. Which prophet did Ahab denigrate to Jehoshaphat, saying, "Did I not tell you that he would not prophesy good concerning me, but evil?"
35. Which prophet's bones brought a man back to life?
36. Whose testimony is "the spirit of prophecy"?
37. Which prophet was a shepherd and gardener?
38. Which prophet was sent to Nineveh to preach?
39. Who prophesied about Edom?
40. Which postexilic prophet was a contemporary of Haggai and encouraged the people to rebuild the temple of Jerusalem?
41. Who prophesied during the reigns of five different kings?

PROPHETIC LITERACY TEST ANSWERS

1. Abraham, Genesis 20:7
2. Balaam, Numbers 22
3. Samuel, 1 Samuel 9–10
4. Nathan, 2 Samuel 12:1–9
5. Ahijah of Shiloh, 1 Kings 14
6. Elijah, 2 Kings 1:9–18
7. Elisha, 2 Kings 2:23–25
8. Saul, 1 Samuel 10:5–6
9. Miriam, Exodus 15:20; Deborah, Judges 4:4; Huldah, 2 Kings 22:14; Noadiah, Nehemiah 6:14.
10. Amos, Amos 7:10–12
11. Hosea, Hosea 3:1–3
12. Daniel, Daniel 2
13. Nahum, Nahum 1–3
14. Zephaniah, Zephaniah 1:12
15. Isaiah, Isaiah 8:3
16. Elijah, 1 Kings 18:44–46
17. Gad, 2 Samuel 24:1–12
18. Isaiah, Isaiah 20:3
19. Daniel, Daniel 1:19—men in the service of ancient kings were often made eunuchs.
20. Ezekiel, Ezekiel 24:16–18
21. Haggai
22. Jeremiah, Jeremiah 38:6–13
23. Malachi, Malachi 3:8
24. Micah, Micah 6:8
25. Ezekiel, Ezekiel 5:1–2
26. Habakkuk, Habakkuk 2:4
27. Jeremiah, Jeremiah 9:1, Lamentations 2:11
28. Joel, Joel 1–2
29. Miriam, Exodus 15:20
30. Deborah, Judges 4–5

31. Samuel, 1 Samuel 10
32. Gad, 2 Samuel 24:11
33. Obadiah, Ahab's housekeeper, 1 Kings 18:1–15
34. Micaiah, 1 Kings 22:8
35. Elisha, 2 Kings 13:20–21
36. Jesus, Revelation 19:10
37. Amos, Amos 7:14
38. Jonah, Jonah 1:2
39. Obadiah, Obadiah 1
40. Zechariah, Ezra 5:1
41. Jeremiah prophesied from the thirteenth year of the King Josiah until the eleventh year of King Zedekiah (c. 627–586 BC, Jeremiah 1:2–3), which also included the reigns of Jehoahaz, Jehoiakim and Jehoiakin.

PART II

PROPHETS 101

1

THE EMBARKATION
The Prophets Can Change Your Life

Sail forth! steer for the deep-water only!
Reckless, O soul, exploring, I with thee, and thou with me;
For we are bound where mariner has not yet dared to go,
And we will risk the ship, ourselves and all.

—Walt Whitman, *Leaves of Grass*

You can throw your body into the struggle and can even let your
blood flow, but that struggle will be in vain, and there will be no
victory if the heart is not in it.

—Michel Quoist, *The Breath of Love*

In 1987 I reached a crucial juncture in my spiritual life, both as
a disciple and as an evangelist. I recognized a need to have my
character overhauled. My quiet and introspective self had to
evaporate. A dynamic and gregarious preacher needed to overcome the subdued one. This change would not come easily. Yet I
was confident that God had brought me to this realization, and he
would see me through.

To fuel the fire of change in my life, I began an intense study
of the prophets of Israel. I knew enough about the prophets to
know that God changed weak and ordinary men and women into

powerful leaders. Amos was a shepherd and a gardener from a small town in the country until God made him into Israel's great social reformer. Jeremiah answered God's call to minister with protests of his youth and inability. Yet God fashioned him into an outstanding religious critic of Judah. Ezekiel was a lonely, isolated priest who lived near the Kebar River in Babylon, until God shaped him into a visionary for those in exile.

God loves to take the ordinary and make it into the extraordinary. He called the prophets in their feebleness and made them firm. Is God's transforming power still available today? Yes—I am a living testimony to this fact. I am not saying that I am by any means extraordinary; but I do know that the prophets turned my life around. I began to dream of having Daniel's conviction, Elisha's power, Ezekiel's intense drive. As I kept these leaders in mind, I became more like them. The prophets had a potent message. Not only can their message turn a shepherd into a prophet, but also a disciple into an evangelist.

A strictly intellectual and academic study of the prophets will not lead to change. We must desire to gain the heart of the prophets by learning the lessons that they taught about their God. These lessons often seem foggy. Because of the unfamiliar language of the prophets, a modern reader can easily get lost. To stay on track as you read about the prophets, ask yourself these three questions: Who is God? Who were the prophets? Who are we?

Who Is God?

The literature of the prophets answers the question, "Who is God?" The prophets vitally understood God's character, and they communicated their understanding of God to the people of Israel. To read the prophets is to get a clearer view of the nature of God.

The ninth through the seventh centuries BC proved to be a time of religious syncretism for the nation of Israel. ("Syncretism" refers to the borrowing of religious practices or beliefs from other sources and blending them into the faith of Israel.) She looked around and desired the kind of king she saw in the bordering nations. Yet to have these kings was not enough. An insatiable desire to be like her neighbors led to the adoption of Canaan's fertility gods: Baal and Asherah. The altars of Yahweh fell into disrepair as new altars went up to the foreign gods with whom Israel had prostituted herself. For example, father and son slept with the same cultic prostitute in the worship of Baal—an abominable situation. The children of Israel even offered human sacrifices to these idols. Consequently, God needed to shake Israel into remembrance.

The Holiness of God

During this time of crisis, the prophetic voice pleaded for Israel to return to her God. Isaiah reminded Israel of God's holiness:

> "Holy, holy, holy is the Lord Almighty;
> the whole earth is full of his glory." (Isaiah 6:3 NIV)

"Holy" means "set apart," and it's no wonder that even seraphs in the heavenly realms felt compelled to say this three times in a row. Majesty, might and power all characterize the God of Israel. Yahweh is the Creator. Since he is the Creator, his creation is to honor him. God brought Israel out of Egypt into a land of promise. God made Israel into a great nation, and he demanded their loyalty. Anything less than total devotion was unacceptable in light of his holiness. God was not another god amongst many gods. Yahweh was and is the God. Israel needed to turn from her adulteries with other gods and return to Yahweh, who was jealous for her. He wanted her to be forever set apart from the sin of the surrounding nations.

The Love of God

Hosea reminded Israel of God's *hesed*: his grace, mercy and love. Israel had been unfaithful to God. She had abandoned him to run after the gods of her neighbors. Would God divorce Israel? Would he leave her to her own destruction, without hope of recovery? No, God's love was long-suffering as demonstrated through his prophet, Hosea.

Hosea's life stands as a testimony to God's love. God commanded Hosea to take a prostitute for his wife, informing him that his wife would not be faithful. Even after she returned to her illicit lover, Hosea was instructed to go and buy her back:

The LORD said to me,
> "Go again and love a woman
>   loved by another man, an adulteress,
> and love her as I, the LORD, love the Israelites
> although they resort to other gods
>   and love the raisin-cakes offered to their
>   idols." (Hosea 3:1 NEB)

Why did God put Hosea through this? It was so that everyone might get a glimpse of the nature of God's love, which is not based on merit. God loves those who do not deserve to be loved. Even when we are at our lowest, ugliest point, God still loves us and desires to have a relationship with us.

The Presence of God

In 587 BC Babylon conquered Jerusalem and took her people into captivity. What was to become of those who were taken into exile by Nebuchadnezzar? In their minds, God's presence was still in Jerusalem. They must have wondered if he would keep them safe in the land of Babylon, miles away from the temple. I'm sure they questioned whether God was still in control of history. These very questions were in the minds of the prophets Ezekiel and Daniel, as well as in the minds of the other Israelites who experienced the Babylonian exile.

The prophet Daniel answered these questions with a solid, "Yes!" Daniel demonstrated that God was in control of every situation. When Nebuchadnezzar threw Shadrach, Meshach and Abednego into a fiery furnace, they escaped without even the smell of smoke clinging to them (Daniel 3:19-27). When Daniel was in the lions' den, God closed the mouths of the lions (Daniel 6:22). Yahweh continued to control all the details. He could handle a big situation and still take care of the fine print. The prophets reassured the people that God's presence was with Israel in Babylon. Just because his presence was not easily felt did not mean that he was absent. God has always been with his people, and he will always be with them.

The Mercy of God

The prophet Jonah confirmed God's desire to forgive people. God longed to forgive the wicked city of Nineveh of her sins against humanity. He prepared Jonah to be his prophet of mercy to the city. As Jonah became this prophet, he learned a poignant lesson about the lengths to which God will go to ensure that people forgive each other. This story is reminiscent of Jesus' teaching on forgiveness:

> "For if you forgive men their trespasses, your heavenly Father also will forgive you; but if you do not forgive men their trespasses, neither will your Father forgive your trespasses." (Matthew 6:14–15)

However, Jonah disobeyed and tried to hide from God because he did not want Nineveh to repent and be saved. But God caused a great fish to swallow the fleeing Jonah. Jonah preached God's important message to Nineveh—and Nineveh repented. What was Jonah's reaction to a whole nation being moved by his message? He was livid and wanted to die! So then God taught Jonah a lesson of forgiveness through a vine. The vine grew up, provided shade for Jonah, and died. Jonah had compassion for the vine and yet had no compassion for the people. God said to Jonah:

> "You have been concerned about this vine, though you did not tend it or make it grow. It sprang up overnight and died overnight. But Nineveh has more than a hundred and twenty thousand people who cannot tell their right hand from their left, and many cattle as well. Should I not be concerned about that great city?" (Jonah 4:10–11, NIV)

The book of Jonah ends with that question ringing through Jonah's head and through our heads. God worked with Jonah to teach him compassion, and Jonah discovered God's mercy in the belly of a fish (Jonah 1–2).

We live in a time of spiritual confusion. Material desires, the latest trends, and Eastern philosophies have become false gods. Hollywood's greatest stars give lip service to God, but their lifestyles remain ungodly. Movies suggest spiritual lessons; yet these messages remain hidden in elaborately woven plots. A voice needs to be heard across the world—a voice that has reached out to offer us help through the centuries. Whose voice? The collective voice of the prophets. God's holiness, God's love, God's presence, God's mercy—all are demonstrated in the prophets. The prophets reveal the nature and character of God. They give us a glimpse of divinity.

Who Were the Prophets?

In times of crisis, a need for dynamic, powerful leadership arises. During the years 1861–1865, the United States of America faced the greatest challenge of her young history. The states were divided in two factions—the North and the South. Civil war threatened to make that divide permanent. To save the Union, a leader was chosen to hold everything together. That leader was Abraham Lincoln.

Lincoln rose to greatness because he faced the challenge when leadership was desperately needed. He had the spirit, the words, the fight and the will to keep the United States united. More books have been written about Abraham Lincoln than any other historical figure, except for Jesus and Shakespeare. What made Lincoln so unique? He stood with conviction in a desperate time.

The prophets of Israel were men and women whom God chose for his purposes in desperate times. They were ordinary men and women with extraordinary hearts. God saw that he could fashion each of them into his instruments to sound forth his message in a time of need. They were not always immediately willing to take up God's charge, but God worked with them, and they became willing. They were not always what they needed to be when God called them, but God changed them into dynamic leaders. What changed the prophets into these dynamic leaders?

The Prophets Saw God

What distinguished the Hebrew prophets from the other religious leaders of their day? What made them different? They saw God. He appeared in their dreams and spoke to them in visions. His presence filled their lives. God's presence was a humbling presence; the prophets never boasted about or flaunted their election. They protested against their calling because of the enormous responsibility that accompanied it. But God himself readied them for their tasks.

Ezekiel was a priest in Jerusalem, taken into exile when Nebuchadnezzar deported the Israelites in 587 bc. His life had been spent ministering to the needs of the Jewish community around the temple in Jerusalem. In exile his job changed. God used Ezekiel to preach a condemning message of woe to the Jews. When Ezekiel began his mission, he was too soft for the job. God had to harden Ezekiel. God told Ezekiel,

> "I will make your forehead like the hardest stone, harder than flint. Do not be afraid of them or terrified by them, though they are a rebellious house." (Ezekiel 3:9, NIV)

His weaknesses then became his strengths.

Similarly, when God first asked Amos to prophesy against Israel, Amos was a sentimental, sappy guy. Amos' response to God's call was, "I cried out, 'Sovereign LORD, forgive! How can Jacob survive? He is so small!'" (Amos 7:2 NIV). Six months later, God asked Amos to raise his fist and strike the altar of Yahweh to symbolize the beginning of God's judgment on Israel. By this time, Amos was ready to obey. From sentimentality to rebellion, then to obedience, God made Amos into what he had to be. Amos followed God's call because once he saw God as he really is, he had to obey—and so must we.

Even a prophet of God can fall, however. The prophet must always remain obedient to God's call. An interesting story about a prophet identified only as "a man of God" from Judah is related in 1 Kings 13. Notice the ups and downs of this prophet's life. He went up to Bethel in Samaria to prophesy against the altar of Jeroboam. He waited until the king was in his presence, and then he foretold the destruction of the pagan altar. Jeroboam was irate at this embarrassing situation. He stretched out his arm, pointed at the man and demanded his arrest. His order did not have the desired effect because Yahweh intervened. Jeroboam's arm froze

in place, extended like that of a police officer stopping traffic.
After that, the altar crumbled to the ground in a pile of dust. The
king begged the prophet to ask for the favor of the Lord concerning his arm. The man petitioned God, and Jeroboam's arm
returned to normal.

Notice the power of this prophet. He stood up to Jeroboam,
the king of Israel, and Jeroboam bowed to his superior power. But
once a prophet sees God and becomes his messenger, he must be
careful to remain righteous. Chapter 13 of 1 Kings continues with
the "man of God" being approached by another nameless
prophet, identified only as "an old prophet in Bethel." The
prophet from Bethel invited his southern compatriot to dinner.
The man of God excused himself by saying,

> "I may not return with you, or go in with you; neither
> will I eat bread nor drink water with you in this place;
> for it was said to me by the word of the Lord, 'You shall
> neither eat bread nor drink water there, nor return by
> the way that you came.'" (1 Kings 13:16–17)

To this the prophet from Bethel responded,

> "I also am a prophet as you are, and an angel spoke
> to me by the word of the LORD, saying, 'Bring him back
> with you into your house that he may eat bread and
> drink water.'" (1 Kings 13:18)

Then the text reads, "But he lied to him."

Why did the old prophet of Bethel lie? Why would he tempt
another prophet to disobey God's command? Was he just testing
the mettle of the man from Judah? Was he seeing what the southern prophets were made of? We do not know. However, we do
know that the prophet from Judah went home with the man, ate
a meal with him and was then killed on his journey south by a
lion. What is the point of this incredible story?

A prophet must remain righteous. The prophet broke a direct
command of God. Yes, he was deceived. Yes, he believed a lie. But
he still broke the command of God. With the vision of the
Almighty came an enormous responsibility. If a prophet could not
live up to his call, he was doomed. James 3:1 reads, "Let not many

of you become teachers, my brethren, for you know that we who teach shall be judged with greater strictness." The prophets of God would certainly concur with this NT statement.

The prophets of Israel saw God. This made them who they were. Can we see God today? Absolutely. Every time we pick up the Bible and read about Jesus, we see God. We have a view of God that the prophets never had: God as fully human, fully divine—God in the flesh. With this revelation comes a responsibility. Since we understand how God lived in this world, we must strive to live as he did while we are here.

The Prophets Stood Up for God

Having seen God, the prophets were compelled to go and speak for him. They took a stand. Often alone and with no hope of companionship, they spoke about what they saw. Jeremiah was told to go to a people who were stubborn and rebellious. God warned Jeremiah about his audience. Jeremiah "previewed" the film, and he knew the ending of the story. Preach hard, preach long, preach with conviction, and preach with intensity—same story every time: the people would not respond. But still, Jeremiah spoke. He could not help but speak. The words burned in his bones like a fire (Jeremiah 20:9). He simply could not contain them.

We could call Ahijah the Shilonite the first prophet of the northern kingdom of Israel. Ahijah prophesied that Jeroboam would receive ten of the Israelite tribes and would become their king (1 Kings 11:30-33). This gave Jeroboam prophetic legitimacy when he made his move against Rehoboam to become king. Yet, when Jeroboam built the high places and left God, Ahijah stood against Jeroboam. In 1 Kings 14 Jeroboam sent his wife in disguise to an aged, almost blind Ahijah. Ahijah recognized Jeroboam's wife and prophesied doom to his house. Ahijah declared the word of the Lord,

> "I will bring evil upon the house of Jeroboam, and will cut off from Jeroboam every male, both bond and free in Israel, and will utterly consume the house of Jeroboam, as a man burns up dung until it is all gone."
> (1 Kings 14:10)

Ahijah stood up to the king of Israel—a man he once anointed—and announced his doom.

Yet another prophet faced off against King Ahab, perhaps the most ruthless in Israel's degenerate line of kings. King Ahab, who did not hesitate to slaughter his own countryman for a vineyard (1 Kings 21), defeated his archenemy, Ben-Hadad I of Damascus, only to grant him pardon. This action violated the idea of God's holy ban.[1] A prophet identified as "a certain man of the sons of the prophets" was called to confront Ahab (1 Kings 20:35). Before the king showed up, the prophet commanded an Israelite to strike him in the face. The bruise was to convince Ahab that he had been in battle. The man refused and was immediately eaten by a lion. Then the prophet commanded another man to do the same, and he wisely obliged. The son of the prophets put a bandage over his eye and entered Ahab's court incognito. He appeared as a soldier coming from battle, requesting Ahab to pronounce judgment because he allowed a prisoner of war to escape from his care. Without any deliberation, Ahab found the man guilty. The prophet "made haste to take the bandage away from his eyes; and the king of Israel recognized him as one of the prophets" (1 Kings 20:41). The prophet pronounced Ahab guilty of allowing Ben-Hadad to escape. This nameless prophet confronted the terror of Israel, and since we have his story, he must have lived to tell about it.

The prophets were men of character and action. They stood up for God against any obstacle. Kings, queens, military leaders, false prophets and foreign gods felt the heat of their conviction. Because of their stand, the ancient traditions of Yahweh continued to live in the eighth and seventh centuries BC in Israel. They were the last bastions of the old ideals of the covenant. They were the torchbearers who kept the flame of Yahwism[2] burning in Israel.

The Prophets Suffered for God

The prophets were known as men and women who would die for their beliefs. Through pain, hunger, sleepless nights and even despite the threat of death, they did not hesitate to preach the

---

[1] The "holy ban" was God's commandment to utterly annihilate an enemy, taking nothing from them in the form of the booty of war. (See 1 Samuel 15:18 -19, for example.)

[2] "Yahwism" refers to the proper worship of Yahweh, the God of Israel.

message of God. Jesus reminded his community of the prophetic legacy at the close of the Beatitudes:

> "Blessed are you when men revile you and persecute you and utter all kinds of evil against you falsely on my account. Rejoice and be glad, for your reward is great in heaven, for so men persecuted the prophets who were before you." (Matthew 5:11 -12)

In connection with persecution Jeremiah comes to mind most readily. He is known as the "Weeping Prophet" because of his anguish over the condition of Israel. He was beaten, put in stocks, publicly humiliated, and cast into a cistern and left for dead. Kings hated him and made numerous attempts on his life. At the end of his life, he was kidnapped and taken to Egypt, where he died in exile away from the promised land. All this happened because he would not compromise God's message.

The most severe time of testing for the prophets was during the reign of Ahab and Jezebel in Samaria. Jezebel declared open season on Yahweh's prophets, hoping to eliminate their presence from Samaria. At the initiation of her holocaust, Obadiah, the keeper of Ahab's household, hid one hundred prophets in two caves, fifty in each cave (1 Kings 18:3–4). During the drought in Israel, Obadiah fed these prophets bread and water so they would survive. We have no evidence of how long these prophets lived under these conditions. They waited for a hero who would deliver them from the hand of Ahab. That hero came in the form of the prophet Elijah, who stood up to the pagan policies of Ahab.

However, the ultimate suffering prophet was Jesus. Centuries before he was born, Isaiah prophesied about the suffering that Jesus would undergo (Isaiah 53). In facing the cross of Calvary, Jesus was one in a great line of prophetic witnesses who stood up for the message of God with their very lives. This line continues down to today.

Who Are We?

As with all Scripture, the message of the prophets strikes us where we live. Often with frightening accuracy, a prophet of the Old Testament can describe our lives as if he or she were living in our own house. As we read the prophets, we must ask, "How does this message apply to me?" More often than not, an answer comes with alarming clarity.

For example, to the disciple who does not give consistently and sacrificially to the church, Malachi writes:

> "Will a man rob God? Yet you rob me.
>
> "But you ask, 'How do we rob you?'
>
> "In tithes and offerings. You are under a curse—the whole nation of you—because you are robbing me. Bring the whole tithe into the storehouse, that there may be food in my house. Test me in this," says the Lord Almighty, "and see if I will not throw open the flood-gates of heaven and pour out so much blessing that you will not have room enough for it." (Malachi 3:8–10 NIV)

To take what we have purposed to give to God and use it selfishly is to rob God. The person who would do this is no better than a thief. Yet we are easily enticed by our own desires and tempted to spend money promised to God on ourselves. We rationalize, thinking, "This is my money; I earned it." God has given us every-thing, and everything is his. Where would we be if God decided to take back the atmosphere around the earth simply because it is his since he produced it? Malachi shows us how we ought to think in this matter. These words stab and sting, but they need to be heard and heeded.

Also, we understand through the prophets that the prosper-ous life is not always the best life. With material gain can come a callous heart and an attitude of superiority. The prophets remind us to keep our hearts soft to the pain, hurt, helplessness and poverty of others.

> Woe to those ensconced so snugly in Zion
> and to those who feel so safe on the mountain of
>   Samaria,
> those famous men of this first of nations
> to whom the House of Israel goes as client.

Make a journey to Calneh and look,
go on from there to Hamath the great,
then down to Gath in Philistia.
Are they any better off than these kingdoms?
Is their territory larger than yours?
You think to defer the day of misfortune,
but you hasten the reign of violence.
Lying on ivory beds
and sprawling on their divans,
they dine on lambs from the flock,
and stall-fattened veal;
they bawl to the sound of the harp,
they invent new instruments of music like David,
they drink wine by the bowlful,
and use the finest oil for anointing themselves,
but about the ruin of Joseph they do not care at all.
That is why they will be the first to be exiled;
the sprawlers' revelry is over. (Amos 6:1 –7 JB)

Once again, a prophet speaks with biting words. He pleads for the cause of the helpless and poor outcast of Israel and against the comfort and ease of the rich. His words beckon people to action, asking them to leave the comfort of their wealth and to work for the welfare of all.

In America's urban centers it is easy to become cynical about the plight of the poor. Homeless people live on the sidewalks, begging for quarters from callous pedestrians. The destitute patch together boxes for housing and rags for bedding. Industrious refugees set up bookstalls beside parking meters to sell the latest "worst sellers" found in the garbage. Their dinner consists of our discarded hamburgers; their dessert is our stale donuts.

Jesus himself said, "'The poor you always have with you'" (John 12:8), but every poor person need not stay poor. Jeff Schachinger, a leader from a Connecticut ministry, related a story to me of a homeless man. When a brother in Christ met this man, he was another one of the nameless homeless people wandering in New York City. He was met in January—a time when the

Modern Sins Addressed by the Prophets

Adultery: Ezekiel 16:32–33; Jeremiah 13:27, 29:23; Hosea 2:2

Bribery: Ezekiel 22:12, Amos 5:12, Micah 7:3

Complacency: Zephaniah 1:12, Ezekiel 30:9

Compromise: Ezekiel 28:18

Dishonest Trade: Ezekiel 28:16; Jeremiah 17:11, 22:13; Amos 8:5–6; Hosea 4:2–3

Extortion: Ezekiel 22:12, Jeremiah 22:17, Nahum 3:1, Habakkuk 2:6

Fearfulness: Jeremiah 1:17, 10:5; Ezekiel 2:6

Flattery: Daniel 11:32, Ezekiel 12:24; 2 Samuel 14:12–21

Giving: Haggai 2:8–9; Malachi 1:7–8, 1:12–14, 3:8

Greed: Isaiah 57:17, Zechariah 9:3, Malachi 3:5

Hatred: Hosea 9:7, Amos 1:11, Obadiah 10, Micah 7:2

Hypocrisy: Ezekiel 13:8–12, 36:19–21; Lamentations 4:12–13, Nehemiah 5:1–13

Idolatry: Ezekiel 6:9, Jeremiah 44:2–3, Micah 5:12–15, Habakkuk 2:18–20

Ignoring the Poor: Jeremiah 5:27–28, 22:15–17; Amos 5:11, 8:4

Immorality: Jeremiah 3:1

Impurity: Ezekiel 23:14–16, 24:13; Jeremiah 4:14; Zechariah 13:1–2

Incest: Ezekiel 22:10–11; Leviticus 18:6–15, 20:17

Ingratitude: Ezekiel 28:12–15, Malachi 2:2

Injustice: Jeremiah 21:12, 22:3–5; Amos 5:7, 5:14–16, 6:12–13

Lack of Discipline: Jeremiah 17:23

Lying: Ezekiel 13:19; Jeremiah 5:2, 12; 9:4–6; Hosea 4:2–3, 7:1

Pride: Ezekiel 28:17, Jeremiah 43:1–2, Daniel 5:20–21, Hosea 5:5, Obadiah 3

Prostitution: Ezekiel 23:8–10; Jeremiah 3:2; Hosea 3:1–3, 4:10; Joel 3:3

Selfish Ambition: Ezekiel 28:5

Self-Love: Ezekiel 28:2; Isaiah 5:8, 56:11

Self-Reliance: Ezekiel 16:15, Jeremiah 43:1–2

Sexual Sin: Ezekiel 22:10–11

Slander: Ezekiel 22:9, 36:3; Jeremiah 6:28, 9:4

Stealing: Hosea 4:2–3, 7:1; Micah 2:2

Stubbornness: Jeremiah 5:3, Ezekiel 2:3–4, Jeremiah 23:17, Hosea 4:16

Worldliness: Jeremiah 5:27–6:20; Deuteronomy 7:3–4, 25

bitterly cold wind freezes the city. "When this man from the street was first invited to the church," Jeff stated, "he was literally living on the floor of Penn Station." From Penn Station, he moved into one of New York's many shelters for the homeless. Then he began to study the Bible. After a few weeks in the shelter, he became a disciple and went out and found a job. Now this man who lived in a cardboard box on the streets of Manhattan lives with brothers and is a responsible disciple, paying his own bills and contributing to the church.

During a recent campaign to raise money for world missions, this brother took to the streets again. This time he went to sell T-shirts that were printed by one of the brothers. I met him on the sidewalk one day as he was selling shirts. He joyously told me that he had raised more than seven hundred dollars for the special missions contribution. I thought about how far he had come: from living on the streets, begging for money to stay alive, to standing in the streets, asking for money to see the world evangelized. I think the prophets would agree that we will always have the poor with us, but the poor do not always need to stay poor.

Today we have an advantage over those who were in the audience of the prophets more than two thousand years ago. We can experience the fulfillment of each message of the prophets in Jesus. He is the message of the prophets lived out. Learning about Jesus through the Scriptures is like seeing a holographic image of exactly what the prophets were looking toward. Much can be learned by applying prophetic teaching to our lives, but the focus is crisper and sharper when the teaching is seen lived out in the life of Jesus.

One question always arises in a study of the prophets: "Must I imitate the prophets in their lifestyle? Am I to live like the prophets?" The answer is "No." We are not called to copy the lifestyles of the OT prophets. Our aim is to be like Jesus—the greatest prophet of all, the ultimate prophet. If we understand Jesus, then we know that he was the most radical prophet to ever walk the earth. His teaching was the most radical ever taught. His life was the most radical ever lived. His community was the most radical ever formed. Should we imitate the prophets? They are mere shadows of Jesus' reality.

Years ago, I formed a group in New York called the "Dead Prophets Society." We got together every so often, and we read together from the prophets. I began every meeting by reading Luke 10:23–24,

> Then he turned to his disciples and said privately, "Blessed are the eyes that see what you see. For I tell you that many prophets and kings wanted to see what you see but did not see it, and to hear what you hear but did not hear it." (NIV)

The prophets would have exchanged seats with any disciple in the twentieth century. We are a part of what they longed to see: the kingdom of God. We have received what they desired to receive: forgiveness. We know him whom they longed to know: Jesus. Should we do what the prophets did? No, in actuality, we should do greater things. Jesus himself said,

> "I tell you the truth, anyone who has faith in me will do what I have been doing. He will do even greater things than these, because I am going to the Father." (John 14:12 NIV)

A lifetime of compelling Bible study awaits us in the lives and preaching of the prophets. As with all study, we will get out of it whatever we put into it. When we understand fully the heart of a prophet, our lives will change. Listen carefully to their voices, and you will hear the voice of Yahweh.

The city screams at mortal terrors created by her own device.
Women walk in fear alone while Satan plays with loaded dice.

No refuge for the homeless.
No sanctuary for the damned.
No playground for the children.
No high plateau or hallowed ground.

Helpless, hapless, hopeless souls are stacked like dominoes for
    the fall.
As mutilated stewards of the abyss await anxiously the
    violent call.
A voice cuts through the empty darkness—piercing, ringing,
    blaring loud.
The whisper of a prophet praying, on bended knees
With countenance bowed.

—G. S. K.

Life Application

1. What do you hope to gain from studying the prophets?
2. In what areas will your character need to change in order for you
to have a prophet's heart?
3. In which of the following areas do you most need to grow in your
understanding: Who is God? Who were the prophets? Who am I?
4. Which prophet mentioned in this chapter most inspires you?
Why?
5. When Ezekiel began his mission, he was "soft." Amos, similarly,
was sentimental. What enabled them to overcome these failings,
and how can you apply the lessons they learned to your own life?
6. What can you learn about remaining righteous from the "man of
God" in 1 Kings 13?
7. How is your heart toward giving sacrificially to the church and
toward having compassion for the physical and spiritual poverty
of others? How can you change it?

2

DEFINING 'PROPHECY'

Shakespeare, the prolific bard of Stratford-upon-Avon, sounded his cry from the rooftops—or at least from the stage of the Globe Theater—by announcing the uselessness of labeling objects that are known intuitively. As his Juliet said, "...a rose by any other name would smell as sweet."[1] What did he mean? Simply this: some words defy definition. This chapter attempts to define the term "prophecy." We will attempt to understand what the ancient Semites meant by this word, and we will endeavor to make the ancient definition of "prophecy" meaningful to us in our day.

In reality "prophecy" defies definition and cannot be summed up by one word or a group of words. It actually had different meanings at different times. Certain Biblical characters had misconceptions about the nature of prophecy. Consider this meeting between Elijah and King Ahab:

> ...Ahab went to meet Elijah. When Ahab caught sight of Elijah, Ahab said to him, "Is that you, you troubler of Israel?" He retorted, "It is not I who have brought trouble on Israel, but you and your father's House, by forsaking the commandments of the LORD and going after the Baalim." (1 Kings 18:16–18, Tanakh)

King Ahab lived in the same predicament that many people find themselves in today. He listened to a false prophet and ignored a true prophet. He saw Elijah as a "troubler of Israel"

54

[1] William Shakespeare, *Romeo and Juliet*, Act II, Scene ii.

because Elijah's words were uncomfortable. Elijah turned Ahab's phrase into fighting words by basically saying, "I'm not the troubler of Israel, but you are. You, your mother and the rest of your family, too!" What is the point? Our perception might be based on misconception, which happens all the time.

For example, when people visit our ministries, they think the church will be the same as any other church they have visited in the past. Some people come ready to be bored to tears. Others come with asbestos suits in case hellfire and damnation rains from the pulpit. Others sit by the aisle, ready to bolt if things get too raucous. A problem exists. People are so settled in what they feel church should be like that they fail to comprehend how God desires his church to be. Our perception is based on our misconception.

Consider how we go about finding a church. We begin to shop around for a church that we think will be enjoyable. One church might have a dynamic preacher but lousy singing—strike one. Another church might have tremendous singing but no fellowship—strike two. Another church might have everything—great singing, great preaching, great fellowship—but no basketball court, strike three. We just struck out.

As a matter of fact, the way we go about finding a church is often backwards. We should not ask ourselves, "What about this church pleases me?" We should rather ask, "What about this church pleases God?" God has already defined the character of his church. It must be devoted to the apostles' doctrine, to the fellowship, to the Lord's supper and to prayer (Acts 2:42). The church must also be a dynamic, growing church (Acts 2:47). If a church does not meet God's qualifications, then it is not God's church. The church we choose might make *us* happy, but will it make *God* happy? We must be careful not to fall into Ahab's trap of wanting to live by our own standard instead of by God's.

In the following section, we will lay out guidelines for defining "prophecy." Then we will place ourselves in ancient Israel to help us to understand how the use of the term differed back then. We will close by attempting to clearly define "prophecy" as it will be used throughout this work.

Defining Biblical Terms

How do we define "prophecy"? What does it mean to prophesy? Does prophecy still exist today? Can we trust the prophecy
of every person who dresses in a frayed robe and stammers
religious jargon? These questions beg for answers. In one sense
"prophecy" defies definition, and until we begin to understand
some of its nuances, it cannot be adequately discussed. The discussion would conclude like the story of the blind men examining
the elephant. Each believed the elephant to be whatever he
touched. The trunk felt like a snake; the leg felt like a tree; and the
side felt like a mountain. As the elephant seemed to the blind
men, so prophecy today means different things to different people. Bernhard W. Anderson, a learned OT scholar, explains:

> Today the term prophecy suggests a variety of meanings. We
> speak of prophets of the weather, prophets of the news,
> prophets who champion a social cause. Even when there is some
> interest in "Biblical prophecy," popular understanding is dis-
> torted by preachers who sometimes give the impression that the
> Biblical prophet gazed into God's crystal ball and predicted the
> shape of things to come. All this is evidence that many of us are
> woefully ignorant of the role of the Old Testament prophets and
> fail to understand properly and appreciate fully the remarkable
> spiritual legacy that we have received from them.[2]

Three different approaches may be used to define prophecy:
defining it from our perspective, looking up prophecy in a modern dictionary and viewing prophecy in its original setting.

Defining "Prophecy" from Our Perspective

Most people today think of prophecy as prediction or prognostication. They imagine a prophet as having the ability to look
into the future and foretell an event before it occurs. Some people
(for example, those from Pentecostal backgrounds) think of
prophecy as ecstatic utterances or emotionally charged speech.
Instead of defining prophecy from a Biblical perspective, they
associate prophecy with their experiential knowledge within their
religious framework.

Biblical terms should not be defined experientially. This is a
prevalent problem in religious circles today. People tend to read the

[2] Bernard W. Anderson, *Understanding the Old Testament*, 4th ed. (Englewood Cliffs, New Jersey:
Prentice-Hall, 1986) 247.

Bible through twentieth century glasses. They do not try to dig into the text to see the cultural setting of a given passage. For some, feelings and experience decide who God is. Therefore they interpret the Bible by listening to their hearts and following their intuition.

What would happen if we consistently approached the Bible with this attitude? Take as an example the Biblical concept of sexual immorality. The Bible uses the Greek word porneia for "fornication" or "sexual immorality." This word had a definite meaning in the first century. Porneia meant "any sexual relations outside of marriage." If we were to define sexual immorality in twentieth century terms, then we would tone down the meaning. Our hearts might lead us to believe that sexual relations are fine with someone we love, whether we are married to them or not. Our experience might tell us that it is fine to have sex outside of marriage with someone as long as it is not destructive or totally self-serving. This kind of thinking could escalate to the point of defining the Bible by human ideas and feelings. In doing so, the Bible no longer is the word of God; it has become the word of man.

Defining "Prophecy" in a Modern Dictionary

Looking up the word "prophecy" in a modern dictionary creates the same problem as the first approach—defining Biblical terms with twentieth century definitions. The English language is continually evolving and changing. The 1611 King James Bible uses terms that are obsolete today. For example, what does it mean to "Gird up the loins of your mind" (1 Peter 1:13 KJV)? Also, the meanings of words have changed. In 1611, "Watch your conversation" meant to watch your lifestyle. Today it means to watch what you say.

To define Biblical terms, we walk two more steps away from modern English. Not only do we take a step back in time, but we also enter another culture and another language. For example, we should not think that the apostle John used the word "love" in his writings exactly as it is defined in Webster's dictionary today. John had several words to choose from when he wrote about love, including *eros, agape* and *philia*. Each of these words has its own nuance of meaning. The only way to know exactly what John meant is to pry into the original text and see which word was used and how it was used.

To illustrate that we cannot rely on just a modern dictionary to define Biblical terms, let's see how one dictionary goes about defining "prophecy" today. The American Heritage Dictionary[3] defines prophecy as follows:

> 1. A prediction. 2. a. The inspired utterance of a prophet, viewed as a declaration of divine will. b. Such a revelation transmitted orally or in writing.

This dictionary goes on to define "prophet" by noting:

> 1. A person who speaks by divine inspiration or as the interpreter through whom the will of a god is expressed. 2. A predictor; sooth-sayer. 3. The chief spokesman of a movement or cause.

Here we see at least three distinct ideas of what a prophet is. The difficulty comes in trying to guess which idea fits within the Biblical text. An even greater problem occurs when we recognize that not one of these definitions might have corresponded to the idea of prophecy in the Hebrew mind of 750 BC, the time of the classical prophets.

Defining "Prophecy" in Its Original Setting

We can define Biblical ideas by viewing words in their original settings. This method yields the most accurate definitions. Any married person can understand how two people are able to view one word in opposite ways. When couples fight, the word "stupid" might be highly offensive to one person. To the other person, it is no more than a casual rebuke. When couples date, "romance" might mean a nice card to one person and a night on the town to the other. The meaning of words in the Bible can also be misconstrued. For example "heaven" could mean the sky, or it could mean the place where God dwells. How should a word be defined? The following four principles should be applied whenever we are looking for the meaning of a Biblical term.

1. Examine the context of the word. The context might define the word in the same passage or in a nearby verse. Proverbs 16:30 states,

[3] *The American Heritage Dictionary*, 3rd ed., ed. Anne H. Soukhanov (Boston: Houghton Mifflin Company, 1992) 993.

> He who winks with his eye is plotting perversity;
> he who purses his lips is bent on evil. (NIV)

What does "perversity" mean? Since this proverb is structured in synonymous parallelism, "perversity" and "evil" have the same meaning. To be perverse is to be evil. Certainly in this case, context helped to define the word.

2. *Use an unabridged concordance.* A concordance will demonstrate how a word is used throughout the Bible, but take into account that the Bible had different authors who wrote at different times and in different countries. Keeping this in mind, a look at the word's usage in other passages might help to make its definition clear.

3. *Look in a Bible dictionary.* A good Bible dictionary is helpful for word studies. The *New International Dictionary of New Testament Theology* surveys the ancient usage of words in the Biblical context. A modern English dictionary is not very helpful in determining a word's meaning in Scripture because it does not include the ancient Hebrew or Greek usage. The Bible dictionary is an invaluable tool in Bible study.

4. *Follow the literal meaning.* A good rule of thumb to follow in defining words is to always give a word its literal meaning unless other considerations prohibit it. Following the literal meaning of a word prevents spiritualizing and allegorizing the scripture to its own destruction.

At times, however, following the literal meaning of words would be senseless. Matthew 8:22 reads, "But Jesus told him, 'Follow me, and let the dead bury their own dead'" (NIV). Jesus gives this answer to a man who wants to bury his dead father before following Jesus. The literal meaning of this verse would be "Let the physically dead bury the physically dead." This is a senseless statement. In reality the spiritually dead should bury the physically dead.

Words are important. One word can change the entire meaning of a passage. Consider the difference between "No" and

"Yes." Also, think about how much difference one letter can make by comparing the words "friend" and "fiend." The r makes a huge difference! "A rose by any other name would smell as sweet." But if you are expecting a rose, and you receive a hose, you will be disappointed. Each word in a passage needs to be carefully defined if the scripture is to be properly understood.

Defining 'Prophecy' in 750 BC

I am a lover of a good science-fiction book or movie. I would wait in line for hours to see the latest space adventure, as I did with the *Star Wars* trilogy. I remember a movie based on H. G. Wells' *The Time Machine* called *Time After Time*. The setting was Victorian England, with all its pomp and splendor. The main character, aptly named "Wells," had just completed his time machine and was waiting for an opportunity to test it. The opportunity was forced upon him when a criminal crashed into his laboratory and entered the time machine as Wells watched. As the authorities arrived, Wells discovered that the criminal was none other than the notorious murderer, Jack the Ripper. Wells had no choice but to enter the time machine and apprehend the criminal.

I believe everyone has visions of time travel. Part of the thrill of watching a movie is being transported to a place and time where you have never been and are not likely to see. Let's take a journey back in time to Israel, 750 BC. The town is Tekoa, a small farm community off the beaten path in Judea. You have spent a long, hard day herding sheep from one pasture to the next. You are ready to call it a night. You have pitched camp, and the coffeepot simmers above the small fire, giving off just enough light to keep the animals away. As you lie down on your wool blanket, you look up and notice that the stars have never looked brighter than they look right then. You sense something mysterious, as if someone is looking at you, but you cannot locate the person in the dark. Suddenly, you hear your name, "Milkiel."

"Yes, who's there?" you answer trembling, as you grab for your staff.

The voice whispers, "Do not be afraid. I have chosen you to speak to my people."

You are puzzled and respond, "Benjamin? If that's you, you're gonna get it!"

"Pay attention, Milkiel," the voice responds with a louder, more serious tone. "You shall be my voice to an obstinate and rebellious people. You will speak, but they will not listen. You are to warn them of the impending judgment to come, but they will not change."

You drop to your knees. Your face pales. You realize that it is the voice of God. Making your voice sound as gentle as a stream, you protest, "But who am I? I am just a small shepherd boy. How can I do your bidding?"

"Today you are no longer a shepherd. Today you are a prophet."

"Fine. Great. Okay. Just one question: What's a prophet?"

This is the question we must answer—but not with what we think a prophet is. So, what was a prophet in 750 BC? How did God define "prophecy" then?

"Prophecy" comes from the Hebrew root *naba'*. There are four views of the derivation of *naba'*:

1. *Naba'* comes from the Arabic root, *naba'a*, "to announce," thus meaning "spokesman."
2. *Naba'* is derived from the Hebrew root, *naba'*, meaning "to bubble up," hence, "to pour forth words."
3. *Naba'* comes from an Akkadian root, *nabu*, "to call," or "one who is called of God."
4. The word is derived from an unknown Semitic root.

Robert D. Culver, an OT scholar, believes that the first suggestion is correct. He writes, "The essential idea in the word is that of authorized spokesman."[4] The prophet was the spokesman of God. He or she served as God's mouthpiece. As Aaron spoke for Moses during the exodus, the prophet served as God's voice to the people.

The Akkadian root *nabu* is found in the text of the prologue of the *Hammurabi Code*, an ancient text pertaining to the kingdoms of Palestine in the days of the prophets. The Babylonian king asserted that he was the *nibit Bel* (called of Baal). He became Baal's

---

[4] Robert D. Culver, *Theological Wordbook of the Old Testament*, ed. R. Laird Harris (Chicago: Moody Press, 1980), s.v. *nabi*, by Robert D. Culver.

viceroy on earth. The Hebrew verb *nibba* signified one who had been appointed to proclaim, as a herald, the message of God himself. This was true of the prophets of Israel.

R. K. Harrison, an OT professor, views the *nabi* (prophet) as being called of God for the express purpose of declaring God's will to his people. "The Hebrew *nabhi*[5] was thus someone who had experienced a vocation or divine call," states Harrison, "and who was fundamentally an independent religious and charismatic figure. He had no hereditary claim to the office, nor could he appropriate the title of *nabhi* by virtue of political appointment."[6] The prophet was called by God; therefore, he had to speak.

Because the *nabi* had a unique relationship with God, he could demand that others seek a closer relationship with God themselves. The role of the *nabi* was to draw Israel back to Yahweh—to the center of her religion. T. H. Robinson, a Hebrew scholar, wrote:

> The *nabhi* was, first and foremost, an enthusiast for his God. To Him he owed his inspiration, and to Him he consecrated his obedience....It was to the prophets more than to any other that Israel owed her learning of her first lesson—"Thou shalt worship Yahweh thy God, and Him only shall thou serve." For it was only on this basis that Israel could learn at all.[7]

The prophets were the last bastions of early Yahwism. Without their voices, the God of Abraham, Isaac and Jacob would have been silenced. They were the voices of Yahweh. Every generation has the potential to let the voice of God sing or be silenced. The history of Israel is a sordid history of frequent disobedience to the voice of God, resulting in a cycle of God's presence and his absence. He was present as his people acknowledged him and apparently absent when they forgot him.

Today we have the same potential—to silence God or to help him sing. God desires to be heard. He has given us his prophets, his word, his church, his Son. But he still needs our voices to be heard. We are his ambassadors, his mouthpieces. Even though we

---

[5] The Hebrew word for prophet is commonly transliterated as *nabi*. Some scholars prefer an alternative spelling, *nabhi*, to designate the same word.

[6] Roland Kenneth Harrison, *Introduction to the Old Testament* (Grand Rapids: William B. Eerdmans Publishing Co., 1969) 742.

[7] Theodore H. Robinson, *Prophecy and the Prophets in Ancient Israel* (New York: Charles Scribner's Sons, 1923) 31.

did not ask for the job, we have it. We need to open our mouths and let God sing.

Biblically Defining 'Prophecy'

The Old Testament is filled with descriptive passages that paint pictures of the life and work of the prophets. Some of these enlighten us about what it takes to be a prophet. Others show us the ways God revealed himself to the chosen spokesmen. Still others help us to appreciate the hardship and struggle that often accompany the call to be an instrument of God.

The Bible also presents material that clarifies the nature of prophecy. These verses help us to define prophecy from a Biblical perspective. One key verse is Deuteronomy 18:14-22:

> You must be entirely faithful to Yahweh your God. For these nations whom you are dispossessing may listen to soothsayers and diviners, but this is not the gift that Yahweh your God gives to you: Yahweh your God will raise up for you a prophet like myself, from among yourselves, from your own brothers; to him you must listen. This is what you yourselves asked of Yahweh your God at Horeb on the day of the Assembly. 'Do not let me hear again' you said, 'the voice of Yahweh my God, nor look any longer on this great fire, or I shall die'; and Yahweh said to me, 'All they have spoken is well said. I will raise up a prophet like yourself for them from their own brothers; I will put my words into his mouth and he shall tell them all I command him. The man who does not listen to my words that he speaks in my name, shall be held answerable to me for it. But the prophet who presumes to say in my name a thing I have not commanded him to say, or who speaks in the name of other gods, that prophet shall die.'
>
> "You may say in your heart, 'How are we to know what word was not spoken by Yahweh?' When a prophet speaks in the name of Yahweh and the thing does not happen and the word is not fulfilled, then it has not been spoken by Yahweh. The prophet has spoken

with presumption. You have nothing to fear from him."
(JB)

Here we find four characteristics of a prophet of Yahweh. Each of these traits demonstrates an aspect of the prophet that sets him apart from the rest of the nation.

1. The prophet must not practice sorcery or divination. This set the prophet of Israel apart from the fertility prophets of the Canaanite religion. The prophets of Baal hoped to coax Baal's blessings through sacrifices, chanting, witchcraft and other forms of enticement. They felt they had to win Baal's favor to keep the forces of nature in check and to produce a harvest. In other words, they thought that Baal had to be appeased to stay pleased.

The prophets of Yahweh knew that Yahweh's favor did not have to be bought or prompted. God had chosen them; they were in his favor because of his selection. He prohibited the use of any of the practices of the pagan religions. There was no need to conjure him up. He had acted in their favor in the past, and he would come to their aid in the future.

2. The prophet of Yahweh must be an Israelite. He must come from among their brothers. This qualification was given to stem the tide of the syncretistic tendencies of the Israelite people. For example, the Israelites saw the nature gods of the Canaanites and adopted many of these gods into their sanctuaries. And while in Egypt, they ate like the Egyptians; after the exodus, they almost turned back to Egypt because they desired food. Not long after their journey into the promised land, they desired a king because the other nations had kings.

God recognized the inconsistency of the Israelites. They were moody. They were up and down. They loved God during times of abundance and doubted him in times of want. The same fickleness characterizes our lives today. Consider "pop" culture. We have a culture that caters to our inconsistency. Fads come and go, yet we buy into each new idea. From Batman shirts to roller blades to "pump up" athletic shoes, we are born suckers. (Imagine a thousand years from now, when an archeologist first digs up a "pump up" athletic shoe. I wonder what he will make of it. He might publish a book entitled, *Weak Ankles and the Fall of Twentieth Century Man*.) Every advertising mogul on Madison Avenue strokes our fickleness. We are the "fad" society.

This fixation on fads is apparent in modern religion. Statistics show that new religious groups begin on the average of three per week in the United States, while established groups close their doors at the same rate. People today desire the new and trendy. New Age religion, Dianetics and Eastern cults all capitalize on the fickle American mind. Many people think that new is better. In religion, "new" is generally just repackaged, regurgitated ideas that have been around for centuries. Usually the appearance of the package, not the quality of the product, is what people buy into.

To keep the children of Israel from following the latest guru of Babylon, God prohibited foreign prophets. This kept in check the weakness Israelites had for fresh, flashy, foreign preachers. And we need to keep the same check on ourselves.

3. *The prophet of Yahweh must speak the word of Yahweh*. The Bible shows us why the prophets were needed. At one time, God spoke to the people directly. He spoke to Adam, Abraham, Moses and Miriam. He spoke directly to the children of Israel through fire and smoke and earthquakes. Yet the theophany[8] of God scared the people. They asked for God not to speak to them directly because they feared for their lives. It was difficult to gaze at the Holy.

Because of the children of Israel's weakness, God gave them prophets who served as his mouthpiece. This supports the idea of the root word for prophet being the Arabic *naba'a*, meaning "spokesman." God gave the prophets his message, and the prophets delivered it—as God's emissaries. John S. Holladay Jr., a Hebrew linguist, writes,

> For all the prophets from Samuel on, that is, from the first individ-
> ual prophet on, there is but one answer to this question of the role
> of the prophet. He was the messenger of Yahweh, God of Israel.[9]

He was called of God and had an audience with God. He was an ambassador from Yahweh. Holladay records the following:

---

[8] A "theophany" is a physical manifestation of God to men.

[9] John S. Holladay Jr., "Assyrian Statecraft and the Prophets of Israel," in *Prophecy in Israel*, ed. David L. Petersen (Philadelphia: Fortress Press, 1987) 123.

> The messenger was an official representative of the sender himself. The royal messenger stood in the court of the Great King, participated in the deliberative processes of the court, received the declaration of the king's wishes from the king's own mouth, and then carried the tablet or sealed roll of papyrus to its destination—in the case of the imperial state administration, to the court of the vassal king.[10]

Similarly, the prophet's authority reflected his position with God. The prophet spoke with authority because his message came from the Creator of the world.

4. *The prophet of Yahweh must pass a test of authenticity.* The test was very simple: if his word came true, then he was a prophet. This test hints at the predictive element, which exists in prophecy. It should be remembered, however, that this predictive element is not the primary characteristic of prophecy. Gleason Archer, a professor of Old Testament studies, states,

> The responsibility of the Old Testament prophets was not principally to predict the future in the modern sense of the word *prophecy,* but rather to tell forth the will of God which the Lord communicated by revelation.[11]

The primary characteristic was speaking the word of God. But this word could contain a statement about the future. (The next chapter will examine in greater detail the role of the prophet.)

Not only does the Old Testament give a test for the authenticity of a prophet, but God also established a punishment for false prophets: death. If this punishment existed today, it would halt the rash prognostications about the Second Coming and the end of the world.[12] Charles Taze Russell, the founder of the Jehovah's Witnesses, missed the prediction about the end of the world several times. He missed it first by picking the date 1914. Then he went on to venture wrong guesses several more times. In the OT days a false prophet would miss a prediction only once! The authenticity of a prophet's call was based on the truth of his oracles.

---

[10] Ibid.

[11] Gleason L. Archer Jr., *A Survey of Old Testament: Introduction* (Chicago: Moody Press, 1974) 296.

[12] See my book, *The Final Act* (Billerica, Mass.: Discipleship Publications International, 2000) for further consideration of end-time prophecy.

We have seen that the proper way to define Biblical terms is by delving into the historical use of the terms in the Biblical text. We looked at the use of the word "prophet" in the eighth and seventh centuries BC, and we looked at the characteristics of a prophet, based on Deuteronomy 18:14–22. As we go on to survey the historical progression of prophets in the Bible, let's take the ideas learned in this chapter with us. A prophet is God's mouthpiece. He is the voice of Yahweh.

The Prophets

Thy Eagle-sighted Prophets too,
Which were thy Churches organs, and did sound
That harmony, which made of two
One law, and did unite, but not confound;
Those heavenly Poets which did see
Thy will and it express
In rhythmique feet, in common prayer for me,
That I by them excuse not my excess
In seeking secrets, or Poetiquenesse.

—John Donne, British poet

Life Application

1. How can you use what you have learned in this chapter about defining Biblical terms like "prophecy" to help you in your personal Bible study?
2. The prophet had a unique role of being God's spokesman and calling others to have a relationship with God. As disciples of Jesus, we also share God's word with others and call them to a relationship with God. How can you better fulfill your role in God's plan?
3. The prophets were clearly set apart by God for his purposes. Is it clear to those around you that you are also set apart and holy? In what areas do you need to change to be less worldly and more like Jesus?

3

SUPERHEROES OR ORDINARY
MEN?

יהוה

Surely the Lord GOD does nothing, without revealing
his secret to his servants the prophets.

Amos 3:7 (NRSV)

The prophet was an individual who said "No" to his society,
condemning its habits and assumptions, its complacency, way-
wardness, and syncretism. He was often compelled to proclaim
the very opposite of what his heart expected. His fundamental
objective was to reconcile man and God.[1]

—Abraham Heschel, Old Testament Scholar

The task of being a prophet seems too difficult for any mere
mortal. Surely the prophets of the Bible were given superhuman
gifts to enable them to accomplish their mission. Maybe they had
vials of oil, which empowered them with the strength of ten men.
Perhaps their endurance was increased with each night given to
prayer. Did they possess rings of charisma or staffs of invincibil-
ity? What enabled the prophets to serve God so powerfully?

We tend to think that the great men and women of the Bible
were superhuman and wonder how could we possibly aspire to
their great faith and courage. To ease this tension, we rationalize

[1] Abraham J. Heschel, *The Prophets,* Vol. I and II. (New York: Harper Colophon Books, 1962) xv.

that they had Herculean gifts to accomplish their mighty acts. How else could Elijah defeat the 850 prophets of Baal and Asherah on Mount Carmel? How else could Elisha's bones bring a corpse back to life?

The answer lies not in the power of the prophets, but in the power of God. The prophets were human, but they served a divine, all-powerful God who worked through them. Many times he worked through them *despite* their shortcomings. They were ordinary people, just like you and me. The prophets often protested God's call, just as we do. They rebelled like we do. Sometimes their faith was strong. At other times, it was weak. They were made of flesh and bones like everyone else.

My wife, Leigh, and I have a son named Daniel. His birth took me back to my youth as I recalled the things I enjoyed doing as a child. I contemplated what we would do together as he grew up: build models, pitch baseballs, throw footballs, watch *Star Trek* and read comic books. I browsed in stores for the old comic books that I used to enjoy. I passed over untouchable superheroes with cosmic or mutant powers like Superman or Iron Man. Who can relate to indestructible humans? I preferred superheroes like Spiderman and Batman. Peter Parker and Bruce Wayne seemed like real people with real lives. They simply had second identities as crime fighters. I could relate to them more.

If we understand who the Hebrew prophets were, then we can relate to them. They truly were ordinary men and women who did extraordinary acts because they served an extraordinary God. What made the prophets unique? How were they able to fulfill their tasks? What was the character of the prophet?

The Prophet As Preacher

A prophet speaks when others remain silent. In the words of Richard Sklba:

> Find something that's right, but perhaps not popular. Find something rooted in the mystery of God, or expressing a true facet of God's will for the world and those who live within it. That's prophetic.[2]

---

[2] Richard J. Sklba, *Pre-Exilic Prophecy: Message of Biblical Spirituality* (Collegeville, Minnesota: The Liturgical Press, 1990) 2.

The message of God burned in the hearts of the prophets. They believed that they had something to say that was from God and must be spoken. They had to cry out this word from Yahweh.

From as early on in the Scriptures as the life of Moses, we can discern that the prophets were preachers. Deuteronomy 18:18 reads,

> "I will raise up for them a prophet like you from among their brothers; I will put my words in his mouth, and he will tell them everything I command him." (NIV)

Moses was a prophet because he proclaimed God's word—he preached. Every prophet after Moses had this same characteristic.

In their days, the prophets were known more for preaching the message of God to their immediate audience than for predicting the future. A noted OT historian, Charles Pieffer, stated:

> Israel's prophets were primarily messengers of God, divinely commissioned to present God's Word to men. The popular concept of the prophet as one who predicts the future is alien to the spirit of Biblical prophecy because it does not describe his true function. The prophet is a spokesman, and it was in this sense that Aaron was termed a "prophet" or spokesman for his brother Moses (Exodus 7:1–2), as Moses was a spokesman for Israel's God.[3]

Moses and Aaron were concerned with revealing God's will to the people in their own situation. When a prophet spoke about the future, it was secondary to communicating the will of God in the present hour.

When the message of God came to the prophets, they had no choice but to declare it. The prophet Amos writes,

> Surely the Sovereign LORD does nothing
> without revealing his plan
> to his servants the prophets.
>
> The lion has roared—
> who will not fear?
> The Sovereign LORD has spoken—
> who can but prophesy? (Amos 3:7-8, NIV)

---

[3] Charles F. Pieffer, *Old Testament History* (Grand Rapids: Baker Book House, 1973) 324.

Jeremiah expressed the same idea by saying,

> But if I say, "I will not mention him
>   or speak any more in his name,"
> his word is in my heart like a fire,
>   a fire shut up in my bones.
> I am weary of holding it in;
>   indeed, I cannot. (Jeremiah 20:9 NIV)

These ideas are at odds with modern views of the prophets as being primarily fortune-tellers or prognosticators. The prophets' primary concern was not the future but the present—specifically the present proclamation of God's will. Walter Zimmerli, an OT scholar, writes, "The prophetic promise proclaims at its deepest level not a coming something, after the manner of the fortune-teller, but He who comes."[4] Another OT professor, R. B. Y. Scott, wrote,

> The prophets were primarily preachers in the highest sense of that term, rather than teachers or prognosticators.... They did make predictions but these were often incidental to their message.[5]

The prophets of Israel desired to communicate the will of God to their contemporaries.

The ministry of Jesus demonstrates this desire. Although at times he did speak about the future, his main concern was to shape twelve men into his image so that they could carry on his work when he was gone. He took care of the lost, sick and outcast, all the while teaching his disciples to do the same. Jesus was concerned with the present.

How did people identify Jesus in his day?

> When Jesus entered Jerusalem, the whole city was stirred and asked, "Who is this?"
>   The crowds answered, "This is Jesus, the prophet from Nazareth in Galilee." (Matthew 21:10–11 NIV)

The crowds could have answered in a number of ways: miracle worker, Messiah, teacher, leader, rabbi. But they saw Jesus as a *nabi*, a speaker or spokesman, because Jesus carried with him the rich legacy of the Hebrew prophets.

[4] Walter Zimmerli, *The Law and the Prophets*, trans. by R. E. Clements (Oxford, England: Blackwell, 1965) 25.

[5] R. B. Y. Scott, *The Relevance of the Prophets*, rev. ed. (New York: Macmillan Publ. Co., 1973) 11.

What the world needs today is preachers who are prophets. My good friend, Mike Taliaferro, is a great example of a prophetic preacher. Mike and his wife, Anne-Brigitte, live in Johannesburg, South Africa, and lead the mission work throughout the entire continent of Africa. Mike loves the Word. I have known Mike for nearly two decades. I have never been with him when he did not have something exciting and fresh to share about his personal Bible study. Mike has inspired me with studies about attacking fear, loving the poor and facing persecution with courage. His sermons, classes and discipleship groups are always crisp. His love for Scripture is contagious. You cannot be around Mike without being challenged about your personal Bible study. We need more men like Mike. His preaching is prophetic.

A prophet must preach. God's message burns within his heart. He will preach to anyone, anytime, anywhere. The prophet is not afraid to declare God's message because he knows it is the truth. Instead, he fears when the message is not preached, for he knows that without the truth, people perish.

The Prophet As Mystic

A prophet sees what others are unable to see. Samuel Terrien has written:

> The prophets of Israel were true poets. They not only cultivated all forms of rhetorical beauty and possessed a respect for the word that provokes thinking, but they also lived in the exultation of their vision.... The prophets of Israel were poets of an electing presence.[6]

The prophets of Israel were preachers who were deeply in touch with God. They were deeply spiritual—dare we say *mystical*. They saw things that other people did not see and dreamed things that other people did not dream.

I am not comparing the prophets to the mystics of Eastern religions. Elijah was no Dalai Lama, nor was Elisha a Tibetan monk. The prophets of Israel were not interested in sitting around in the lotus position with upraised palms chanting, "Ohmmm, ohmmm, ohmmm." They were contemplative, but their contemplation led to action within their communities, not seclusion from community.

---

[6] Samuel Terrien, *The Elusive Presence: Religious Perspectives* (New York: Harper & Row Publishers, 1978) 227-228.

They were mystical in the sense that they viewed the world differ-
ently from their compatriots—they saw God's hand in everything.
Who would say that Ezekiel was not a mystic? How can the wheel-
within-a-wheel vision of Ezekiel 1 be explained except as a mystical experience? Ezekiel saw God in that vision. To receive a revelation from God is out of the ordinary—it is mystical.

Daniel was a mystic by this definition. He saw things that
other people did not see. The vision he received in Daniel 11 was
extraordinary. He described a cosmic battle being waged between
the king of the North and the king of the South. The setting, par-
ticipants and details of this battle remain unclear. The outcome of
the battle was clear: God won the victory. The prophets were
poets and visionaries. They had an edge to them that other people
did not have. They were deeply spiritual—mystical.

In Deuteronomy 13:1 the prophet is defined as one who fore-
tells by dreams. The Biblical term for this is "seer." Samuel, the
judge and prophet, was a seer. One Biblical story tells how the
young Saul sought out Samuel. He wanted him to discern the
location of his father's lost donkeys—not the noblest task a
prophet was ever asked to tackle. God spoke to Samuel in a
dream, revealing not only the location of the donkeys but also that
Saul was destined to be the first king of Israel (1 Samuel 9:15-17).
When Saul sat down to eat with Samuel and his friends, no one
except the prophet noticed anything unique about Saul. Samuel
saw a king. God's revelation enabled Samuel to view things dif-
ferently from everyone else.

Consider how Balaam received his prophetic oracles:

> "The oracle of Balaam son of Beor,
>   the oracle of one whose eye sees clearly,
> the oracle of one who hears the words of God,
>   who has knowledge from the Most High,
> who sees a vision from the Almighty,
>   who falls prostrate, and whose eyes are opened"
> (Numbers 24:15 –16 NIV)

Balaam dreamed the dreams of God and envisioned God's
visions. The eyes of the prophet are opened to see the world in a

unique and special way. He does not see things as the rest of the world sees them. He recognizes God's control over history.

There were occasions when the Spirit of God would overwhelm a prophet, placing him in an ecstatic trance. This even happened to King Saul, although it is not clear if his experience entitled him to be considered a prophet or not:

> So Saul went to Naioth at Ramah. But the Spirit of God came even upon him, and he walked along prophesying until he came to Naioth. He stripped off his robes and also prophesied in Samuel's presence. He lay that way all that day and night. This is why people say, "Is Saul also among the prophets?" (1 Samuel 19:23 –24 NIV)

God's Spirit overwhelmed Saul. He disrobed and lay in an ecstatic trance, prophesying for a full day and night. Although this element of prophecy is not highlighted in the Hebrew tradition, it did exist. The prophet could be swept away by the Spirit to prophesy as the Spirit saw fit.

None of this is to say that the prophets were simply mediums of God. They were men of this world, involved in this world and concerned about this world. They had both personality and character. They were spiritual leaders who walked with the Spirit. To say that they were mystics is to say that they walked with God. They walked, talked, breathed and lived God.

T. H. Robinson compares a prophet to a physical scientist. He writes:

> It was his [the prophet's] to study the mind of God in his dealings with men. He had to discover the Divine attitude towards human relationships, an attitude expressed not in an arbitrary system of rewards and punishments, but in a reasonable chain of cause and effect. To him was granted the insight, born of direct communication with God, to see with startling clarity that a given type of conduct, still more a given attitude of the soul, carried within itself the seeds of prosperity or disaster.[7]

The prophet was a student of everything holy. He walked in communion and in communication with God. This spiritual perspec-

---

[7] Theodore H. Robinson, *Prophecy and the Prophets in Ancient Israel* (New York: Charles Scribner's Sons, 1923) 46.

tive caused him to have a totally different point of view from the rest of the world.

Anyone who desires to be a prophet must have this mystical quality about him or her. They must see God in everything. The toppling of the Berlin Wall and the dismantling of the Soviet Union is not just history running its course; it is God's hand opening up the Eastern Bloc countries to receive his word. The rampant crime in the inner cities of the United States is not just a matter of urban blight; it is Satan's attack on the major population pockets in our country. The prophet sees a cosmic battle raging. It is the battle between light and darkness, good and evil. The prophet feels that he is on the front line, fighting with God to destroy the forces of darkness. The battle stokes his intensity. It fuels his passion. It arouses his righteousness.

When I think of a modern day mystic, I think of Henry Kriete, a brother and friend, who preaches in Norfolk, Virginia. Henry and his wife, Marilyn, walk the mystical edge. Henry loves God. He seeks to draw near to God in unique ways. Once, as I visited Henry in Bombay, India, he told me about putting together a makeshift telescope to look at the stars. As he looked at the stars, he contemplated the greatness and majesty of God. Henry has gone into the woods of his native Canada and danced before the Lord. Once he planned a date with Jesus. He fixed a meal, put out an extra plate and had supper with Jesus. He carried on a conversation with Jesus throughout the meal. He even asked Jesus to disciple him and to challenge his character. Henry Kriete is a mystic. He has not shaved his head, adorned orange robes or walked barefoot over hot coals (not as yet, anyway). But he sees things that other people do not see. He sees God's hand in everything.

The Prophet As Prognosticator?

This seems like a good place to digress and chase a worthy rabbit. How do we relate the idea of prophecy as the preaching of revealed truth with the predictive element of prophecy? Is prophecy more preaching or prediction?

First, let me state clearly that prophecy does contain a predictive element. True prophecy can contain a telling of the future. It is not my intention to disclaim the predictive nature of prophecy.

My intention is to place this predictive element in its proper context—within the bigger picture of prophecy.

We all know religious groups that emphasize the future side while neglecting the practical truths expressed in prophecy. How many preachers scan the book of Daniel for glimpses of the end of the world only to miss the spiritual lessons taught there? The books of the Minor Prophets speak as boldly to our lifestyles today as do any of the other parts of Biblical literature. Yet, often the relevant message in these books is overlooked as the expositor strains to emphasize the next sign for the end of time.

The OT prophets were not mere prognosticators. "Psychic" Jeanne Dixon and the prophet Isaiah have nothing in common. The prophets of Yahweh were not interested in being clairvoyant. They were interested in revealing the truth about God. Samuel Terrien, who has developed a theology of God's presence, states, "The prophets of Israel unveiled not the future but the absolute."[8] Richard Sklba writes,

> The truth of the matter is that the prophets of Israel did not predict the future because they were too busy giving expression to the present. Like poets of all ages, they saw reality at its deepest level.[9]

The task of the prophet was to present God, not the future.

Yet there were times when God revealed the future to a prophet. In fact, one test for the validity of a prophet was the trustworthiness of his prophecy. As early as Deuteronomy 18 we read that the measure of a prophet's message was its accuracy. A "wait and see" attitude could determine the prophet's worth: when he prophesied about the future, the people would "wait and see" if the prophecy came true. If it did, he was a prophet of God. If not, then he was executed as a false prophet.

The Old Testament is full of references to the predictive nature of prophecy. The ephod and the sacred lots (Urim and Thummim— Leviticus 8:8) were used by priests to determine God's voice in particular matters. They were instruments of divination, used to call upon God to reveal his will in certain situations.

[8] S. Terrien, 227.
[9] Sklba, 2.

Some prophets possessed distinctive psychic gifts. Elisha discerned plans made in secrecy miles away (2 Kings 6:12). R. K. Harrison wrote,

> Sometimes the prophets received their inspiration by means of dreams and visions, the significance of which could be perverted through indulgence in wine or liquor (Isaiah 28:7). Under certain conditions there was clearly some sort of mystic element present in their self-projection.[10]

These elements of prophecy do not negate the fact that most prophecy in the Old Testament simply revealed a specific message from God. The attempt to see the future everywhere in Biblical prophecy is not new. Throughout the centuries many men have tried to predict the end of the world. These predictions have often been based upon scriptures found in the OT prophetic writings. Some of the predictions are as follows:

- Ignatius, Polycarp, Justin and Irenaeus, of the second century AD, and Hippolytus of the third century, said that the world would end five hundred years after the birth of Christ.
- Lactantius, of the fourth century AD, said that judgment was at hand.
- Otto of Freising, in 1100 AD, said that the world would end in 1260. Joachim of Flora set that same year as the "age of the Spirit" in his book, the Eternal Gospel.
- Militz of Kroneriz set the date between the years 1365–1367.
- During the Reformation period, Hoffman the Anabaptist set the year as 1533.
- H. Gratten Guinness, in Light of the Last Days (1888), picked the year as 1930.
- Charles Taze Russell, the founder of the Jehovah's Witnesses, in his Millennial Dawn (1907), said that the world would end in 1914.
- Bill Dawson picked 1934 in his The Time Is at Hand (1926).

What do all these men have in common? They guessed, and they guessed wrong. According to Deuteronomy 18, they would all be worthy of death. If this punishment were carried out for

[10] Roland Kenneth Harrison, *Introduction to the Old Testament* (Grand Rapids: William B. Eerdmans Publishing Co., 1969) 754.

every incorrect prognostication, then the margin of error would rapidly begin to drop.

In the main, Biblical prophecy is concerned with the here and now. God spoke through the prophets in order to inform their contemporaries as to how they should live. To miss this is to miss the central element of prophecy.

The Prophet As Radical Reformer

A prophet acts while others sit and watch. Long before the fictional "Starship Enterprise" ever flew her first mission, the prophets of God already had decided to boldly go where no one had gone before. The prophets broke new ground. While they took up the mantle of their predecessors, they often ascended to a higher level of intensity. They were radicals.

Many of history's most inspirational leaders have been radicals. They are people who will do things that others only talk about. In 1987 my wife, Leigh, and I made our first trip to India. Our dream was to lead a church planting to New Delhi. While we were in Delhi, we visited the spot where Mohandas K. "Mahatma" Gandhi was assassinated. Gandhi was a great leader. Although there are qualities about him that I do not admire, there is no denying that he was a radical. In his drive for home rule of India, he went to any extreme (short of violence) to make his point. He led marches to the sea, initiated strikes that shut down the entire country, lived like the people and fasted for peace. In 1947, the world's focus was on him. He single-handedly stood opposed to the British oppression of Indian citizens. He was willing to be imprisoned, to be beaten and to die for his cause. Whether we appreciate Gandhi or not, we must admit that he was a radical.

Obviously, one can be radical without proper knowledge and wisdom, which brings damage (Romans 10:2). Nonetheless, the serious follower of God will be a radical. In what ways were the Hebrew prophets radical? What can they teach us about having a radical spirit?

1. *The prophets stood against kings, priests, society and other prophets.* Before the rise of the monarchy in Israel, judges ruled

over a tribal confederation. One such judge was Deborah, who was also a prophetess. She sat under the Palm of Deborah in the hill country of Ephraim, and the people came to her for advice. At that time King Jabin of Hazor led the Canaanite forces to battle against the Israelites. Sisera was the commander of Jabin's army. Deborah grew tired of the hardships that the Canaanites placed on her people. She called Barak and asked him to gather all the forces of Israel together for war. Barak agreed, but only if Deborah would accompany him. Deborah answered Barak,

> "I will surely go with you; nevertheless, the road on which you are going will not lead to your glory, for the Lord will sell Sis´era into the hand of a woman." (Judges 4:9)

Deborah was radical. She was willing to do what others would not try. While everyone was steeped in self-pity or complacency, she took a stand. She led the forces of God to wondrous victory and left behind a song of praise to commemorate the event (Judges 5).

By the time of the classical prophets (the written prophets, 750–550 BC), the social and political structure in Israel had solidified. At the head of the government was the king. Surrounding the king was his court, which consisted of counselors, advisers and prophets. At the head of the religious cultus was the high priest. Surrounding him were priests, musicians and prophets. Therefore, the prophet had risen to a legitimate position in Israelite society.

History teaches that once something becomes widely accepted, it is easily corrupted. For example, see how some radicals of the 1960s in America became corporate moguls of the 1990s. Once the prophetic office in Israel became accepted, it also became corrupt. Instead of declaring the message of Yahweh, the court prophets bowed to the influence of the kings. The court prophets would preach peace when there was no peace (Jeremiah 6:13–14). But God still had a faithful few in the land. These prophets took a stand against the "official" voices and declared the true message of God. They were the voices of Yahweh.

Jeremiah had his share of trouble with the leaders of his day. King Jehoiakim gathered around him a number of prophets who would declare whatever he wished to hear. Jeremiah had other ideas. He prophesied directly against the throne of Jehoiakim and against these false prophets. In the fourth year of Jehoiakim's reign, the word of God came to the prophet Jeremiah. His secretary, Baruch, recorded it in a scroll and read it in the Lord's temple. Later, it was taken to the king.

> It was the ninth month, and the king was sitting in the winter house and there was a fire burning in the brazier before him. As Jehu 'di read three or four columns, the king would cut them off with a penknife and throw them into the fire in the brazier, until the entire scroll was consumed in the fire that was in the brazier. (Jeremiah 36:22 –23)

Many prophets would have given up at this point—but not Jeremiah. He dictated a second scroll to Baruch, which contained everything the first scroll did and more.

Jeremiah was just as courageous with the religious powers of his day. Jeremiah 28 records the contest of Jeremiah and the false prophet, Hananiah. Hananiah prophesied that Israel would soon return home from captivity. Jeremiah opposed Hananiah and prophesied that he would be dead within the year. Two months later, Hananiah was dead.

The Hebrew prophets squared off against the status quo of their day. They were the radical, antiestablishment, longhairs of Israel. Their views did not make them popular, and they were especially unpopular in the eyes of the kings and their courts. But the prophets never sought to win any popularity contests. In spite of the rigors, they preached an unpopular message to a stubborn, rebellious people.

2. *The prophets were willing to suffer and die for their cause.* Many people will talk and protest. Even more will talk of protest and do nothing. But few will suffer and die for a cause. The prophets of Israel were known for their suffering. Hardship and rejection were commonplace in their lives. Through their pain they continued to

carry out their purpose. They spoke God's message because it burned on their hearts.

Jeremiah is the greatest example of a prophet who suffered. He ran into hardship at every turn. This did not quiet his voice, however. The men of Anathoth plotted to kill Jeremiah to shut him up (Jeremiah 11:18–23). The false prophet, Pashhur, had Jeremiah beaten and put in stocks at the Upper Gate of Benjamin at the temple, where he became a public spectacle (Jeremiah 20:1–6). King Jehoiakim targeted him as a public enemy and plotted his death (Jeremiah 26). Later, King Zedekiah threw Jeremiah into a cistern and left him for dead (Jeremiah 38:1–13). Jeremiah's life was a life of sacrifice. He gave himself to a people who despised and rejected him.

I cannot help but think about the lives of the apostles in the New Testament. They suffered as prophets. Jesus warned them that they would suffer (John 15:20). They had a model of how to hold up under suffering: Jesus himself. They could think of their Master as they faced the stones, swords and crosses. They could also think of the prophets and be inspired by their courage.

In Acts 4, Peter and John were arrested for preaching about Jesus. The Jewish officials in Jerusalem commanded them not to speak. They answered the officials as prophets would answer,

> "Whether it is right in the sight of God to listen to you rather than to God, you must judge; for we cannot but speak of what we have seen and heard." (Acts 4:19 –20)

Prophets throughout the ages have spoken what God put upon their hearts and have suffered because they spoke.

3. *The prophets used prophetic symbols to express God's message.* Symbols were used throughout Bible times to emphasize a message. Sometimes the signs were as simple as a person stooping over to draw in the dirt (John 8:6) and sometimes as elaborate as naming a newborn son, "Not my people" (Hosea 1:9, 2:23). A sign (Hebrew *oth*) could be given in a supernatural way, or it could come from the creative genius of the prophet. Bernhard W. Anderson explains the use of signs by writing,

In the Bible a sign does not stand by itself; rather, it is closely linked to the prophetic word, as in Isaiah 7. The purpose of a sign is to make visible, to confirm dramatically, the truth and power of Yahweh's word spoken by a prophet. The sign does not have to be a stupendous miracle, in our sense of the word, for its significance is not so much its unusual character as its power to confirm a prophetic word spoken in threat or promise.[11]

The prophets were masters at using signs, symbols and gestures to illustrate their message. The signs of the prophets varied. Elijah's choice of clothes—sandals and a garment made of hair (2 Kings 1:8)—illustrated that he was a man of the desert. This reminded the Israelites of their desert experience at Sinai and God's covenant with Israel. Jeremiah purchased a linen belt. Instead of wearing it, he placed the belt in a crevice where it would become soiled (Jeremiah 13:1–11). After the belt was ruined, he wrapped it around his waist as a symbol of the ruined state of Judah. Imagine the disgusted stares, turned-up noses and cold shoulders Jeremiah received as he paraded around Jerusalem in a soiled, smelly belt. He may not have made many friends this way, but he made his point.

Isaiah was another bold prophet who preached in the time of Assyrian dominance. These ruthless warriors deported whole cities back to Assyria, leaving the towns in ruins. To transport the prisoners, they lined individuals in single file, stripped off their clothes and sandals, and chained them together by placing hooks in their buttocks. Needless to say, no one attempted escape.

To illustrate the condition of an Assyrian prisoner of war, Isaiah walked around Jerusalem naked and barefoot (Isaiah 20:1–6). He did this to create alarm. He wanted God's people to know that the Assyrians were going to take captive their sometime allies in North Africa. He lived like this for three years! Isaiah paraded around Jerusalem naked and barefoot as a prophetic symbol of the coming judgment of God. Can you imagine what his wife and children must have thought of this? We usually do not think of the prophets as being married, but many of them were. In fact, Isaiah's wife was a prophetess (Isaiah 8:3).

[11] Bernhard W. Anderson, *Understanding the Old Testament,* 4th ed. (Englewood Cliffs, N.J.: Prentice-Hall, 1986) 331.

The most radical aspect of Isaiah 20 is that Isaiah performed this sign not for the Israelites, but for the Egyptians and Ethiopians who were about to be attacked by Assyria. That Isaiah would put himself through such an extreme situation for three years for an enemy of Israel is astonishing. This illustrates the lengths to which God will go to demonstrate his love to people.

The prophet most well known for his prophetic gestures is Ezekiel. The genius of Ezekiel is demonstrated by the dramatic acts that illustrated his message. Notice some of the unusual acts that Ezekiel performed as prophetic gestures:

- Ezekiel 2:9–3:3—Ezekiel eats a scroll produced by God, and it is as sweet as honey.
- Ezekiel 3:22–27—Ezekiel is placed in solitude by God. Even his tongue clings to the roof of his mouth so that he will not prophesy.
- Ezekiel 4:1–8—Ezekiel builds a model of Jerusalem and lies down before it to symbolize its siege. He lies 390 days on one side and 40 days on the other side, totaling 430 days.
- Ezekiel 5:1–6—Ezekiel shaves his head and cuts his beard with a sword. He takes the hair and teaches a lesson with it.
- Ezekiel 6:11—Ezekiel claps his hands, stomps his feet and cries out to get the attention of the people.
- Ezekiel 12:1–16—Ezekiel packs up his belongings and goes to a wall, digs through the wall and at dusk walks away from his audience. The next day he returns to the wall and pronounces doom against Jerusalem.
- Ezekiel 24:15–24—Ezekiel is told that his wife, who is his delight, will die. He is instructed not to mourn or grieve for her. This is a symbol of how the people must act when the temple is destroyed.
- Ezekiel 37:15–28—Ezekiel takes two sticks of wood (one for the northern kingdom of Israel and one for the southern kingdom of Judah), and he makes these two sticks look like one. This symbolizes the restoration of the two kingdoms into one nation of Israel. It also contains messianic undertones.

This is just a partial list of the prophetic signs that Ezekiel performed. As with Isaiah, it is important to remember that Ezekiel was married when he performed some of these strange acts. We should not think of Ezekiel as some wild-eyed lunatic who ecstatically carried out these acts. These gestures were a mark of inspiration, not lunacy. They were performed, not to bring attention to himself, but to underscore his message. If more preachers today would put the same time, thought and effort into their lessons that Ezekiel did, then no one would complain of church services being boring! People want to experience the word of God being brought to life.

When I think of a modern day radical, I think of Mark Templer, who now lives in London, England. Mark and his wife, Nadine, worked in India for years building the ministry there and teaching the disciples how to serve the poor. I love to hear Mark pray. He screams to God with loud cries and tears—and his zeal never wavers. He gives a spark of life to everything he touches. Mark has learned how to stay excited through tough times. His life has been threatened again and again. In Bangalore, an enemy of the church even paid an assassin to kill him. When Mark heard about the assassin, he did not head back to the United States, flashing his passport to every official along the way. Instead, he prayed for strength and continued preaching. Mark will always be preaching. If he reaches ninety and has a choice of whether to take a break or preach—Mark will preach. He is a radical man, and in that way, he has the spirit of the prophets.

While the prophets inspire us and teach us, our purpose in life is not to imitate the prophets. We have a higher goal—to be like Jesus. We should remember that no prophet preached as powerfully as Jesus, suffered more than Jesus or lived more radically than Jesus. Today men and women who wish to change the world must be willing to pay the same price. They must have the message of God burning so fervently in their hearts that it must be preached. For this to take place, two things must happen.

First, we must drink deeply of God's word. How can we truly preach the message of God with conviction unless we love the Word? Our hearts must desire the word of God. We should feel inadequate if we have not spent quality time in the Word. Verses should be going through our heads all day long. In life, if we want to know how much someone loves us, we watch how much energy he or she gives toward helping us achieve our dreams. If we love the Word, we will give our whole heart to it. The Word, in turn, will give us a whole heart.

Second, we must preach. If we love the Word, then we will share our enthusiasm with others. Anything we are excited about, we talk about. When we get engaged, we naturally talk about our fiancées to anyone who will listen. If we are about to have a baby, we find ourselves sharing our joy with the most unlikely stranger. The excitement of the event activates our mouths, and we cannot keep quiet. If we are inspired by the Word, it will be natural to share our love for it.

When we love the Word and preach the Word, we become like the prophets. The more we become like the prophets, the more we become like Jesus. This should be our ultimate goal in life—to be like Jesus.

Life Application

1. The prophets were passionate about God and his word. What can you do to make your personal Bible study and drawing near to God exciting and fresh?

2. Do you drink deeply of God's word? Is your love for Scripture contagious? To your Bible discussion group? In fellowship? In family devotional and discipling times?

3. Would the people around you say that you are deeply spiritual? Do you walk in communion and communication with God?

4. The prophet's "spiritual lifestyle caused him to have a totally different point of view from the rest of the world" (p. 72). Do you recognize God's control over history? What does this quote mean to you in terms of trusting God in current events?

5. If you have a leadership role, are you an inspiring leader? Do you do what others only talk about? What can you learn from the prophets and from Jesus in having a radical spirit?

6. If you lead family devotionals, a Bible discussion group or teach the Bible in a public setting, do you put the kind of creativity and effort into your teaching and examples as Ezekiel is described in the Bible as putting into his lessons to the people?

PART III

A SURVEY OF THE PROPHETS

4

FROM THE PATRIARCHS
TO THE JUDGES

The prophet is not only a prophet. He is also a poet, preacher,
patriot, statesman, social critic, moralist.

—Abraham Heschel, Old Testament Scholar

When I was in the tenth grade, I hated literature. "Disgust" is
too light of a word; "hate" is the right word. During English class,
I either caught up on my sleep or practiced the fine art of making
paper airplanes. All this changed when my class began studying
Greek mythology. These superheroes with their larger-than-life
stories grabbed my attention. Mercury, Mars, Apollo and Athena
kept me from failing tenth-grade English. They also taught me to
love literature.

It did not take me until the tenth grade, however, to learn to
love the Bible. As a small child, I was fed a steady diet of the
exploits of the great men and women of the Bible. Family devotionals and Sunday school classes taught me the stories of Daniel,
Jonah, Elijah and Elisha. God's "superheroes" taught me to love
God. More specifically, the prophets of Israel showed me who
God is.

To comprehend what the prophets say about God, we must
first discern the role of the prophet. Our primary understanding
of the character and function of a prophet comes from what we
know of the classical prophets of the eighth and seventh centuries
BC. For most people, this can be truncated to an understanding of

the four major prophets (Isaiah, Jeremiah, Ezekiel and Daniel) and a couple of the minor prophets (Amos and Hosea). This abridged understanding is unfortunate because the Bible presents a rich and colorful portrait of the prophets of God, beginning with Abraham and running throughout the Scriptures. As the following list demonstrates, prophetic figures were present on numerous occasions in the Bible:

1. The first designated *nabi* was Abraham (Genesis 20:7).
2. Some prophets were part of a dancing, ecstatic "band of prophets" who roamed the countryside (1 Samuel 10:5).
3. Prophets could be individual seers (1 Samuel 9:9).
4. Prophets could be national leaders (1 Samuel 7:3–17).
5. Special prophets were royal advisers (2 Samuel 7:1–17).
6. Some kings maintained a circle of court prophets as consultants to the government (1 Kings 22:6).
7. Israel was blessed by the classical prophets of the eighth and seventh centuries BC (mentioned above).
8. Jesus was the ultimate prophet (Matthew 21:10–11).
9. There were prophets in the first century church (1 Corinthians 12:27–31).

In this section, we wish to survey the role of the prophet throughout the major time periods of the Bible. We will begin with the Patriarchal Period, the time from creation to the giving of the law on Mount Sinai. Next, we will survey the material between Moses and the rise of the monarchy. Because of the importance of Samuel in the development of the prophetic office, we will study the rise of the monarchy in chapter 5. In chapters 6 and 7, we will consider the period of the charismatic prophets, with Elijah and Elisha as the main characters. To complete our survey, we will briefly consider the period of the classical prophets (750-550 BC), as well as the role of the prophet in the New Testament, in chapter 7.

This historical examination will provide a sweeping overview of the history of the Biblical prophets. It can also serve as a character study of some of the great men and women of the Bible. As we survey the lives and work of these prophets and prophetesses, we will make practical spiritual applications along the way. The purpose of this overview is to help us to understand the importance of the prophetic role throughout the whole of the Bible. By understanding this role, we will have a greater appreciation for the role of the prophet in classical prophecy.

The Patriarchal Period

The Patriarchal Period is the time from the creation to the giving of the law on Mount Sinai. It is called the Patriarchal Period because during this time, God communicated his will to humanity through the heads of the households, the patriarchs. Adam, Enoch, Noah and Abraham all belonged to this period.

When I think of the Patriarchal Period, I am transported back to my childhood. I think of rainy afternoons spent looking through an old Bible storybook with desolate paintings of gray-haired men with long beards who were surrounded by sheep. I think of days when I wanted to don a pith helmet and khaki pants to go exploring in ancient worlds to find the tomb of Jacob or Esau. Is it possible to learn from the patriarchs without choking on dust? Absolutely. We must take God's will as revealed to them and apply it to our own time.

God decided to set his plan of redemption into motion early in human history by choosing one man through whom the world would be blessed. Thus Abraham became the father of the faithful. God placed him in a unique role, making him God's first prophet, his spokesman. In Genesis 20, Abraham is called "a prophet" by God himself. Abraham lied to Abimelech, king of Gehar, telling him that his wife, Sarah, was actually his sister. He feared that Abimelech would desire Sarah for his own. Abimelech was informed in a dream about Abraham's deception. God declared to the king, "'Now return the man's wife, for he is a prophet, and he will pray for you and you will live'" (Genesis 20:7 NIV). Therefore, in spite of his weaknesses, namely, his lack of trust and his deceitful heart, God designated the man and then made him into what he needed him to be. Abraham, the father of the faithful, became Abraham, the father of the prophets.

The Bible also mentions Abraham's grandson Jacob as being a prophet. Jacob was never given the designation "prophet," as was Abraham, but his actions were prophetic. Genesis 49 catalogues the blessings of Jacob for his sons. As Jacob blessed his son Judah, he prophesied about the Messiah,

> "Judah, your brothers shall praise you:
> you grip your enemies by the neck,
> your father's sons shall do you homage,
> Judah is a lion cub,
> you climb back, my son, from your kill;
> like a lion he crouches and lies down,
> or a lioness: who dare rouse him?
> The scepter shall not pass from Judah,
> nor the mace from between his feet,
> until he comes to whom it belongs,
> to whom the peoples shall render obedience." (Genesis 49:8-10 JB)

Jacob prophesied about Judah's future and the future of all of Abraham's descendants. The nation of Israel was not in existence yet, but its royal lineage was already pronounced. God spoke through Jacob, establishing Judah as the tribe from which David would rise to power and later through which Jesus would come. God chose Jacob to be his spokesman of this future truth.

From Moses to the Monarchy

After the death of Jacob, the fate of God's people was sealed through Joseph and his brothers living in Egypt. Generations passed, and the descendants of Abraham became slaves to the oppressive power of the Egyptian pharaoh. What happened to God's plan? How would a dynasty be built of slaves? God would use a prophet. Enter Moses. Walter Bruggemann, author of *The Prophetic Imagination*, notes,

> I would urge that we are on solid ground if we take as our beginning point (in a study of the prophets) Moses as the paradigmatic prophet who sought to evoke in Israel an alternative consciousness.[1]

[1] Walter Brueggemann, *The Prophetic Imagination* (Philadelphia: The Fortress Press, 1978) 15.

Do you remember Charlton Heston's portrayal of Moses in *The Ten Commandments*, with flowing robe and staff in hand, standing at the edge of the Red Sea, watching the Hebrews cross as the Egyptian army quickly closed in upon them? Those scenes made movie history. More important, those scenes made salvation history.

In many ways Moses was the preeminent prophet of the Old Testament, yet he was also much more than a prophet. Moses was a priest, judge, seer, intercessor, lawgiver, miracle worker and prophet. Walter Eichrodt, an OT theologian, states,

> Justice, then, can never be done to the full historical reality, if the attempt is made to imprison this outstanding figure in any of the ordinary categories of holy men.[2]

Moses transcended normal categories. He was responsible for the salvation of God's people from Egyptian domination. The Ten Commandments and the record of the early history of the Hebrew religion would be lost except for Moses. Deuteronomy 34:10–12 closes the Pentateuch with this description of Moses,

> Since then, no prophet has risen in Israel like Moses, whom the LORD knew face to face, who did all those miraculous signs and wonders the LORD sent him to do in Egypt—to Pharaoh and to all his officials and to his whole land. For no one has ever shown the mighty power or performed the awesome deeds that Moses did in the sight of all Israel. (NIV)

Moses was greater than the prophets because he did not communicate with God in visions and dreams—he communicated with God face to face (Numbers 12:8).

Other prophets lived during Moses' lifetime. Aaron, the brother of Moses, was a prophet. He was Moses' spokesman, and in that way, he was also God's spokesman. Exodus 7:1–2 states,

> Then the LORD said to Moses, "See, I have made you like God to Pharaoh, and your brother Aaron will be your prophet. You are to say everything I command you, and your brother Aaron is to tell Pharaoh to let the Israelites go out of his country."(NIV)

[2] Walter Eichrodt, *Theology of the Old Testament*, Vol. I, trans. J. A. Baker (Philadelphia: The Westminster Press, 1961) 290.

Aaron was the mouthpiece of Moses, nothing more and nothing less. They shared a unique relationship, just as Moses shared a unique relationship with God.

Moses' sister, Miriam, was a prophetess. She led the women in celebration of Yahweh's great victory over the Egyptians.

> Then Miriam the prophetess, Aaron's sister, took a tambourine in her hand, and all the women followed her, with tambourines and dancing. Miriam sang to them:
>
> > "Sing to the Lord,
> >   for he is highly exalted.
> > The horse and its rider
> >   he has hurled into the sea." (Exodus 15:20 -21 NIV)

The Bible bears witness to the rich tradition of women who spoke for God, beginning with Miriam. She was a role model for the other Israelite women. The "Song of Miriam" is one of the most beautiful songs of praise in the Bible. Yet she was more than a role model or songwriter; Miriam was a prophetess. She was chosen out of all the men and women in the Israelite camp to speak on God's behalf. Miriam prophesied because God called her to be his voice.

Consider one other scripture in the Mosaic context of the prophets. Numbers 11:1–30 presents Moses as a troubled leader who was weighed down by the demands of the people. The children of Israel's constant bickering and complaining grated on Moses until he was beginning to despair. Moses went to God for help. God told Moses to gather the seventy elders of the people at the Tent of Meeting. When the elders gathered, God placed his spirit on Moses and the seventy elders, and they prophesied. Two of the elders, Eldad and Medad, were away from the Tent of Meeting when the spirit came. They began to prophesy in the camp, to the astonishment of the people and to the concern of Joshua. Joshua ran to Moses. He told him about Eldad and Medad and pleaded with Moses to stop them from prophesying. Moses responded to Joshua, "I wish that all the Lord's people were prophets and that the Lord would put his Spirit on them!" (Numbers 11:29 NIV).

Two facts about prophets can be learned from this interesting story. One, Moses validated prophets and demonstrated the need for them. Since the prophets received of the same spirit as Moses did, they spoke with the same authority as Moses. The fact that God "spoke" through his law is tremendous, but God still needs men and women to speak for him. He looks for people to share his work, and he is willing to provide them with the ability to be effective for him.

Two, the prophets were united by God's spirit. They shared the same spirit and the same purpose. A sense of unity exists between true prophets of God. Moses did not worry about the two elders left in the camp because they had the same spirit as the other sixty-eight. In fact, Moses wished for everyone to have that message and that spirit. True unity would exist if this were the case.

The classical prophets, such as Isaiah and Ezekiel, could reach all the way back to Abraham to substantiate their heritage. But to get a vision for the spiritual quality and effectiveness of their role, they looked to Moses as the prophet par excellence.

A very early view of the role of the prophets of God is found in the story of Balaam (Numbers 24). Balak, king of Moab, was distressed because Israel had defeated the Amorites, and he surmised that Moab was next in line. Balak sent for Balaam, to inquire through him of God's purposes. At first God was not going to allow Balaam to prophesy to the Moabites. But God relented and Balaam delivered four oracles to Balak. The third oracle gives an insight into the character of a prophet. Numbers 24:15–16 reads,

> "The oracle of Balaam son of Beor, the oracle of the man with far-seeing eyes, the oracle of one who hears the word of God, of one who knows the knowledge of the Most High. He sees what Shaddai makes him see, receives the divine answer, and his eyes are opened."
> (author's translation)

The prophet sees and understands events as God does. Guided by spiritual insight, he rejects the thought patterns of society, acknowledging God's hand in everything that happens.

Included in the prophets before the monarchy was Deborah, one of the great female prophets of the Bible. As the children of Israel began to settle the promised land, a need for leadership became manifest. God raised up judges to provide guidance for his people during tough trials, one of whom was Deborah. She led Israel to victory over Sisera and the army of Canaan.

The first reference to Deborah in the Scriptures refers to her as a prophetess. Judges 4:4 states, "Deborah, a prophetess, the wife of Lappidoth, was leading Israel at that time" (NIV). Like Miriam, Deborah led her people in song. The "Song of Deborah" in Judges 5 is a magnificent praise to Yahweh for his victory in battle.

> "When the princes in Israel take the lead,
>   when the people willingly offer themselves—
>   praise the LORD!
>
> "Hear this, you kings! Listen, you rulers!
>   I will sing to the LORD, I will sing;
>   I will make music to the LORD, the God of Israel."
>   (Judges 5:2–3 NIV)

Long before the era of the written prophets, God's Spirit was at work in men and women who were chosen to be his mouthpiece. From the time of Abraham and the patriarchs, through the period of the judges, we remember the names of otherwise ordinary people for one predominant reason—they were the voice of Yahweh.

Life Application

1. How has this chapter expanded your view of and appreciation for prophets?
2. Moses was a powerful prophet who spoke with God "face to face." How does this man's walk with God inspire you? What do you need to change to become more like Moses?
3. Several of the prophets mentioned in this chapter had several roles. What are some of your roles? Are you glorifying God with these roles? Are there any roles you need to eliminate or alter so that you can be more effective?
4. How does it make you feel to know that God used prophetesses as well as prophets (e.g., Miriam, Deborah)? Does this change your view of or vision for the women in your life?

5

SAMUEL AND THE RISE OF THE MONARCHY

יהוה

It was the best of times, it was the worst of times, it was the age of wisdom, it was the age of foolishness, it was the epoch of belief, it was the epoch of incredulity, it was the season of lights it was the season of darkness, it was the spring of hope, it was the winter of despair, we had everything before us, we had nothing before us, we were all going direct to Heaven, we were all going direct the other way—in short, the period was so far like the present period, that some of its noisiest authorities insisted on its being received, for good or for evil, in the superlative degree of comparison only.

—Charles Dickens, *A Tale of Two Cities*

My grandmother, Carrie Mae Kinnard, always told me that she lived through the most dramatic period in human history. She was born in 1903 ("The same year as Bob Hope," she would note proudly). She witnessed the change from horse and carriage to the automobile. She observed men take to the air in planes, and then watched them travel in space to walk on the moon. The invention of radio and television came during her lifetime. I can only imagine the shock she received seeing her first "talking picture show." Those were electrifying days.

The most dramatic period of Israel's history was the time of the rise of the monarchy. How exciting it must have been to see a loose connection of tribal states unite under one leader to become a mighty nation! What a thrill to see the anointing of the first king of Israel and then to see him eclipsed by an even brighter king.

How exhilarating to witness the rise to power of a kingdom that would have an influence in the Middle East for centuries.

In the Hebrew Bible, the books of Joshua, Judges, Samuel and Kings are called the "Early Prophets" or "Former Prophets." (The books of Isaiah, Jeremiah, Ezekiel and the twelve minor prophets are known as the "Later Prophets.") The role played by the prophets who appear in the Early Prophets—Samuel, Gad, Nathan, Elijah, Elisha, Isaiah, Jeremiah and others of lesser note— is considerable. The book of Kings provides us with the historical background for the ministry of the pre-exilic, "writing" prophets. These books and prophets also have much to say about events related to the rise of the monarchy.

Samuel

Samuel was the last judge of Israel. He was also a prophet. Samuel brought Israel from the time of the judges into the beginnings of the monarchy. As a prophet, he served as a bridge from the early traditions of prophecy to the later tradition of the classical prophets. (The differences between the role of a prophet in these two time periods will be clarified later on in this work.) During his lifetime the *nabi* fulfilled at least four different roles in Israelite society: (1) professional seer—1 Samuel 9; (2) leader of a community of seers—1 Samuel 10:5-6, 2 Kings 2:3-4; (3) ecstatic prophet—1 Samuel 10:5-6, 19:19-24 and (4) religious functionary—such as the court prophets opposed by Jeremiah.

Chapters 9 and 10 of 1 Samuel describe the role of the prophet at the rise of the monarchy in Israel. Saul, the future king of Israel, began a quest to find his father's lost donkeys. As Saul was about to abandon his mission, his servant told him to inquire of Samuel, a man of God. Samuel could tell him where the donkeys were. Saul protested, saying he had no money to give to Samuel. But the servant possessed a quarter of a shekel of silver, which he insisted would suffice as payment. They went in search of the prophet. God had informed Samuel of Saul's presence, and Samuel went to find Saul. When Samuel identified Saul, he told him that God had chosen him to be king over Israel.

This story proves interesting in many ways. Saul sought Samuel to pay him for the service of discovering where the lost donkeys were. This means Samuel was a professional seer. As a seer, God enabled him to see things that other people did not see. By the time of David, it became commonplace for prophets to be paid for their services—for example, the court prophets who served the king. It is interesting to note that as early as Samuel's time, men made their living from prophecy.

Saul's story does not stop here. Samuel goes on to anoint Saul as the king over Israel. To verify Saul's anointing, he tells him to travel to Gibeah:

> "After that you will go to Gibeah of God, where there is a Philistine outpost. As you approach the town, you will meet a procession of prophets coming down from the high place with lyres, tambourines, flutes and harps being played before them, and they will be prophesying." (1 Samuel 10:5 NIV)

By the ninth century, some of these professional prophets, of whom Samuel was one, had banded together in groups. John Bright, a respected OT scholar, describes these groups as follows:

> We find groups of them living a communal life (2 Kings 2:3, 5; 4:38–44), supported by the gifts of the devout (4:42), often with a master at their head (6:1–7). They were distinguished by the mantle of their office (2 Kings 1:8; cf. Zechariah 13:4) and apparently also by a distinctive marking (1 Kings 20:41). They would give their oracles in groups (1 Kings 22:1–28) or singly (2 Kings 3:15), elevated to ecstasy by music or dance and for these they would usually expect a fee (2 Kings 5:20–27, cf. 1 Samuel 9:7f.). Their demeanor caused many to think them mad (2 Kings 9:11); now and then they were the object of jeers (2:23–25). They were, however, zealous patriots, following the armies of Israel in the field (3:11–19), encouraging the king to fight the nation's wars (1 Kings 20:13f.), and desiring that these be conducted according to the rules of Holy War (vv35–43).[1]

The prophets were becoming a part of the religious structure in Israel. As the priesthood existed within the fabric of society, the prophets were now becoming an integral part of it as well. By the time of Elijah, not only had the prophets of Yahweh united into

[1] John Bright, *A History of Israel*, 3rd ed. (Philadelphia: Westminster Press, 1981) 248 -249.

accepted groups, but the false prophets of Baal had been assimilated into the social structure as well.

The prophets of Israel were not just charismatic leaders after the tradition of Abraham, Moses or David. Samuel certainly was a great charismatic leader, but he also was part of a class of religious functionaries (temple prophets or prophets of the king's court) whose purpose was to serve the people and meet their needs. By the mid-eleventh century BC, the prophets had become a recognized part of the religious environment. Even before the temple was constructed, bands of prophets roamed the lands to minister to the people of Israel.

Nathan

During his kingship, Saul brought together a weak band of tribes and gave them cohesiveness and unity. But when David became king, everything in Israel changed. David inherited Saul's unity and took Israel to a position of power. The king became the leader of Israel—politically, militarily, economically (taxes) and even religiously. He gathered around him a court of royal advisers—consisting of soldiers, priests, sages and prophets—to help him administrate the land.

In 2 Samuel 7 David sought advice from his court prophet Nathan concerning the ark of Yahweh. David lamented, "'Here I am, living in a palace of cedar, while the ark of God remains in a tent'" (v2 NIV). That very night, the word of Yahweh came to Nathan, informing him that David would build a spiritual house for Israel that would last forever. This is a great example of the role of the court prophet. He would seek the counsel of God to either validate or cancel the plans of the king. He was a true adviser to the king. (How great it would be if this practice could be restored to our political system today!)

The court prophet also guided the spiritual welfare of the king. After David sinned with Bathsheba and had Uriah killed, his heart was callous. 2 Samuel 12:1 states, "The LORD sent Nathan to David." Nathan shrewdly confronted David in order to show him his sin. He revealed to David a moving story of injustice between a rich man and a poor man. David's anger sizzled. At this, Nathan turned to

David and said, "You are the man!" (v7). God used Nathan to rebuke David, to soften his heart and to bring him to repentance.

The role of the court prophets was important. Bernard W. Anderson comments on their role:

> Regarded as experts in prayer, particularly intercessory prayer, they were called upon to bring the people's petitions before Yahweh. Moreover, as Yahweh's spokespersons, they communicated the divine answer to a particular petition, or indicated whether or not an offering was acceptable to the deity.[2]

The prophet was to seek the counsel of God in order to guide the king in his decisions. If the court prophet was unrighteous, then the entire kingdom would suffer. This is exactly what would happen later in Israel.

Gad

Gad is distinguished in the Scriptures as being both a prophet and "David's seer" (2 Samuel 24:11). When David took a census of his fighting men, he realized he had sinned against the Lord. David petitioned God in prayer to find a way of reconciling his wrong. God did not answer David directly. He sent his answer through his prophet Gad, the court seer. Gad had to deliver an unpleasant message to the king. As court prophet, he had to face the pressure of declaring the truth or saying what the king wanted to hear. This required for him to be a man of courage and conviction.

Ahijah

Later, as the kingdom of Israel was about to be split into two separate kingdoms (Israel in the north and Judah in the south), Ahijah the prophet predicted that the division would happen. He told Jeroboam that he would lead ten of the tribes as their king. Later in Jeroboam's reign, Jeroboam sought out Ahijah to prophesy about his son's sickness. He sent his wife, in disguise and bearing gifts, to inquire of Ahijah about their son. The Lord informed Ahijah of her impending visit, declaring that as soon as she set foot across the threshold of the palace, her son would die. Ahijah declared the message of Yahweh; "I will burn up the house of Jeroboam as one burns dung, until it is all gone" (1 Kings 14:10 NIV).

---

[2] Bernard W. Anderson, *Understanding the Old Testament*, 4th ed. (Englewood Cliffs, New Jersey: Prentice-Hall, 1986) 252.

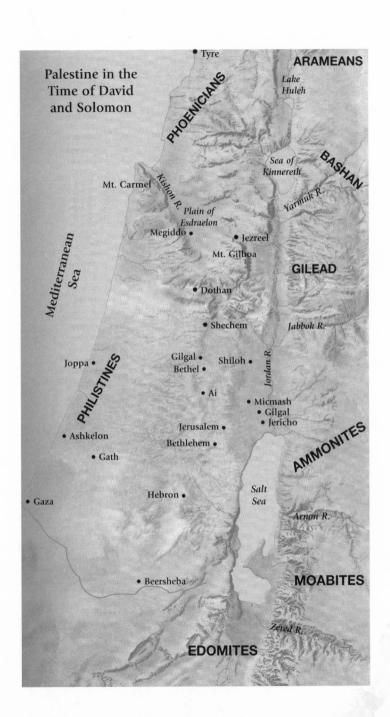

Palestine in the
Time of David
and Solomon

Tyre

ARAMEANS

Lake
Huleh

PHOENICIANS

BASHAN

Sea of
Kinnereth

Mt. Carmel

Kishon R.

Plain of
Esdraelon

Yarmuk R.

Megiddo •

• Jezreel

Mt. Gilboa

GILEAD

Mediterranean
Sea

• Dothan

• Shechem

Jabbok R.

Joppa •

Gilgal •

Shiloh •

Bethel •

Jordan R.

PHILISTINES

• Ai

• Micmash
• Gilgal
• Jericho

Jerusalem •

• Ashkelon

Bethlehem •

AMMONITES

• Gath

Salt
Sea

• Gaza

Hebron •

Arnon R.

• Beersheba

MOABITES

Zered R.

EDOMITES

Imagine the courage it took for Ahijah to inform the king of his son's death and the demise of his dynasty! Not everyone who claimed to be a prophet of Israel possessed this courage. Courage was one essential quality that separated a true prophet from a false one.

After the division of the kingdom of Israel between Rehoboam and Jeroboam, the prophets played a prominent role in the court of almost every king of Israel and Judah. This important development was due, in large part, to the heroic work of Samuel and the prophets of the united monarchy.

Life Application

1. The court prophet advised and directed with intercessory prayer. Who have you been advising and counseling lately? Have you sought God's will through intercessory prayer, or have you relied mainly on your own wisdom and insight?
2. Gad had to "face the pressure of declaring the truth or saying what the king wanted to hear" (p. 104). Do you proclaim the truth or simply tell people what their itching ears want to hear? How can you change to be more of a modern-day prophet in this area?
3. How can you imitate the courage of these prophets?

6

THE CHARISMATIC PROPHETS

Elijah

יְהוָה

As I write this chapter, I am in the process of reading Douglas Southall Freeman's *Lee's Lieutenants*. After Freeman completed his Pulitzer prize-winning *R. E. Lee*, he turned his attention to recording the history of other great Confederate leaders in the Civil War. Freeman was puzzled about how to present the other commanders of the war without them being overshadowed by Lee's prominence. In the introduction to his work he recorded, "A question plagued and pursued: In holding the light exclusively on Lee, had one put in undeserved shadow the many excellent soldiers of his army?"[1]

Similarly, the rise of the charismatic prophet in Israel in the ninth century was dominated by three powerful Biblical figures—Elijah, Micaiah and Elisha. By charismatic, I mean that these prophets were known because of their dynamic personal charisma. They were also great miracle workers. The work of these prophets was so significant that they almost overshadow all the prophets who preceded or succeeded them. These men set the standard of righteousness, power and charisma for the later classical prophets.

The charismatic prophets differed from the classical prophets in that they were oral prophets who did not record their prophecies in writing. We have records of them because someone else recorded the events of their lives carefully, preserving for us the

[1] Douglas Southall Freeman, *Lee's Lieutenants*, Vol. I (New York: Charles Scribner's Sons, 1943) xv.

words that they spoke. Elijah and Elisha alone deserve hours of study. Their charismatic personalities make them two of the most beloved of Biblical characters.

This chapter chronicles Elijah's life, while Micaiah and Elisha are discussed in chapter 7. To better understand who Elijah was, I have given the following synopsis of his life based on the Biblical text. I hope you will read the Bible verses and follow the notes presented in this text. In addition to teaching about Elijah, it is my prayer that it will serve as a practical example of the kind of deep Bible study you can learn to do on your own.

1 Kings 17:1–19:18—Elijah came from Gilead, east of the Jordan River, on the edge of the desert. Gilead was a territory that Israel settled; it was uninhabited by earlier Canaanite civilizations. This was the seat of Patriarchal Yahwism, and Elijah was upset at the syncretism west of the river.

Elijah had lived the rough, tough, seminomadic life on the edge of the desert. He must have looked out of sorts in the city of Samaria with his garment of hair, leather belt and strange diet of locusts and wild honey (2 Kings 1:8).

1 Kings 17:1–7—The battle begins. Elijah entered the scene when Israel was at her lowest point spiritually. What approach would he take against the political and religious authorities? Would he try to come in through the back door by means of a sneak attack? No, Elijah engaged the battle. He challenged Ahab by initiating a drought in the land. Since Baal was the Canaanite god of rain, this was a direct affront to his divinity. Yahweh would test Baal.

Elijah retired to live near the brook, Cherith, east of the Jordan River. Ravens came to his aid, supplying him with meat and bread. Elijah trusted God, and God came through for him. This theme is seen throughout Elijah's life. If you trust God, he will come through.

1 Kings 17:8–16—When the brook dried up, God directed Elijah to a widow's house in Zarephath in Phoenicia. The woman was almost out of meal (flour) and oil when Elijah arrived. Because of Elijah's blessing, God supplied her with meal and oil until the drought ended. The widow trusted God, and he came through.

God controlled the weather, not just in Israel, but in the neighboring countries as well—even in Phoenicia, where Baal Melkart should have ruled. This underscores the fact that Yahweh, the God of Israel, is the true God who controls nature.

1 Kings 17:17–24—The widow of Zarephath called upon Elijah because her son had died. Elijah prayed for the boy, and he came back to life. This mighty act confirmed his message to the widow. She responded, "'Now I know that you are a man of God, and that the word of the LORD in your mouth is truth.'" Although she trusted before, her faith was increased. The widow kept trusting God, and God kept coming through.

1 Kings 18:1–15—Obadiah was in charge of King Ahab's palace. He was a devoted believer in Yahweh. During the drought in Israel, Jezebel ordered the assassination of all the prophets of Yahweh. Obadiah gathered a hundred prophets together and hid them in two caves. He fed them from the stores of King Ahab. If he had been discovered, he would have paid with his life, but he trusted God.

Obadiah was sent on an errand by the king when he happened upon the prophet Elijah. Elijah told Obadiah to go and announce that he would visit the king. Obadiah questioned this command and basically said, "If I tell the king that you will come and you don't, then I will die. I have been faithful to God. Why ask me to perform this task since it could end in such calamity?" Obadiah nonetheless trusted God, and he went to the king.

Faith is not blind. If we obey God without any sense of why we are obeying, then we will never learn. Maturity comes from understanding. It is okay to ask, "Why?" The question does not negate the obedience. Obadiah trusted. He trusted with questions, but he still trusted. He trusted, and God came through.

1 Kings 18:16–40—This passage records the showdown on Mount Carmel. Beginning with King David, an element of foreign religion began to creep into Israel. One hundred and fifty years after David, while King Omri was on the throne, the situation worsened. Omri founded Samaria as the central seat of the government. He opened the floodgate for Israel's neighboring countries to contaminate the land. When Jezebel of Tyre married Ahab, Omri's son, the cult of Baal was accepted into the palace. Those who worshiped Yahweh now found themselves on the defensive.

Jezebel's influence changed the course of history for Israel. Bernard W. Anderson writes,

> The French writer Pascal once said that the whole course of Western history was changed by the shape of Cleopatra's nose. We might say that the course of Israel's history was profoundly affected by the eccentricities of one person, Jezebel.[2]

To accommodate Jezebel, Ahab built a "Temple of Baal" in Samaria. Baal was Baal-Melkart, the official deity of Tyre, and the god of fertility. Jezebel was an aggressive, domineering woman who had a plan to see Baal worship suffocate the traditional religion of Samaria. She imported the prophets of Baal from her homeland and paid them out of the temple treasury. She wreaked havoc on the followers of Yahweh—tearing down Yahweh's altars, killing his priest and driving the faithful into seclusion.

Elijah arrived on the scene to champion the cause of Yahweh. On Mount Carmel he faced off against 850 prophets of Baal and Asherah—one man against an overwhelming majority. But Elijah had God on his side. The prophets of Baal called upon their deity by working themselves into a frenzy. They danced around, leaping from one foot to another, shouting the name of their god. When Baal did not respond, Elijah began taunting them:

> "Cry aloud, for he is a god; either he is musing, or he has gone aside, or he is on a journey, or perhaps he is asleep and must be awakened." (1 Kings 18:27)

This fueled their fire. They slashed themselves with swords to get their god's attention.

Here we learn that zeal is no substitute for the truth. Just because a person is intense—full of conviction and fire—does not mean that he is right. The prophets of Baal mutilated themselves for a false god. Truth is reasonable, not emotional.

The severity of Israel's apostasy was demonstrated by the condition of the altar of God. Before Elijah could even offer his sacrifice, he had to repair the altar of Yahweh. Elijah demonstrated who the real God of Israel was by calling down a fire from heaven to utterly consume the altar. The people saw this and exclaimed, "Yahweh—He is God! Yahweh—He is God!" The people once again learned to trust God. Elijah awakened their faith through a demonstration of God's power.

Their trust led to obedience. Elijah led the people in the slaughter of the 850 prophets of Baal and Asherah. Elijah called his people back to the roots of their Hebrew religion. The death penalty for apostasy, as stated in Exodus 22:20, was carried out. Elijah was determined that Israel throw off the shackles of foreign, idolatrous religions and return to her ancient ways.

1 Kings 18:41–46—Yahweh brings the rain. Whenever you trust God, he will come through. The people trusted and God delivered rain. After the victory on Mount Carmel, Elijah further fortified Yahweh's supremacy over Baal by calling an end to the drought. A cloud appeared from the sea, which became a storm. He informed Ahab of the coming rain and sent him ahead in his chariot to Jezreel. Elijah ran to Jezreel, seventeen miles away, beating Ahab's chariot back to the city.

1 Kings 19:1–21—Elijah went on to champion the cause of Yahweh in various ways, but he first had to weather a storm himself. Elijah is portrayed with superhuman qualities in the Bible. Rain fell at his command, and he ran ahead of the king's chariot for seventeen miles. In spite of these accomplishments, Elijah also suffered the pain, emotion and frustration that come with being human. After his great victory on Mount Carmel, Elijah felt empty and alone:

> He came to a broom tree, sat down under it and prayed that he might die. "I have had enough, LORD," he said. "Take my life; I am no better than my ancestors." (1 Kings 19:4 NIV)

He was afraid. Jezebel had made him public enemy number one. He went from the heights of victory to the valley of despair. He was human, and his humanity made him doubt. But even in his doubt, God did not give up on him. God showed Elijah his presence in the midst of his seeming absence.

Feeling God's absence, Elijah went to Horeb, the mountain of the Lord. He wished to place himself in God's presence. God asked Elijah why he was there. Elijah could have found God at any point along his journey, not just at Horeb. God still had work for Elijah to do, so why was Elijah taking the time to go all the way to Horeb when God was actually with him every step of the way?

God passed by Elijah, and Elijah saw his procession. God was always on the march, always moving, never stagnant. But God did not manifest himself to Elijah in the way that Elijah assumed that he would. God was not in the earthquake, fire or wind—the old manifestations of theophany. He spoke in a gentle whisper. The proper translation would be: in a silence so quiet that you could hear it.[3] God was different from Elijah's preconceived ideas about him. He came to Elijah in a way Elijah did not expect.

This reminds us of Jesus—a man who could never be pegged, pigeonholed or tied down. He was a king, but not the king everyone was expecting. He was powerful, but his power came in a surprising form. Jesus was the fulfillment of OT law. He took that same law and nailed it to a cross, nullifying its authority. Jesus did not fit anyone's mold. Likewise, God was not predictable for Elijah, nor is he for anyone today.

Elijah overcame his doubts, and in 1 Kings 19:15–18, he was the first prophet to mention a remnant being left in Israel. God sent Elijah to anoint new kings and a new prophet. These men would help purge Israel of fake gods by putting people to death. God announced, "Yet I reserve seven thousand in Israel—all whose knees have not bowed down to Baal and all whose mouths have not kissed him" (v18 NIV). What an infinitesimal minority in Israel were recognized by God as his own—yet, that is the nature of a remnant. God works through a small number of faithful people to call the world back to him. Elijah anointed Elisha to later succeed him.

1 Kings 21:1–29—The story of Naboth's vineyard once again pitted the Yahweh-fearing prophet against the insatiable apostate Ahab. Naboth rejected Ahab's bid to buy his vineyard. He

---

[3] Anderson, 276.

insisted, as was his legal right under the Deuteronomic law, on keeping his family property. Being a Hebrew, Ahab recognized these rights. Thus, he was downcast and depressed. God had instituted the rights of the individual within his society. Even the king himself could not ignore those rights.

Jezebel, Ahab's wife, differed. Being a Canaanite, she held the king to be supreme over the individual or the society. He was the embodiment of god and could make the claims of a god. If a man stood in the king's way, then he must die. Thus, Naboth was marked for death.

This was not just a clash between Elijah and the king, but was representative of the conflict between traditional Yahwism and the syncretistic religions of Canaan. Hebrew law upheld the right of the individual, protecting him from the wealthy landowner or the greedy tyrant. As Elijah stood against the status quo, so too, would Amos, Micah and Isaiah stand against the tyranny of the rich.

2 Kings 1:1–8—Although Ahab and Jezebel attempted to kill Elijah, he survived both of them. After Ahab's death, his son, Ahaziah, took the throne. Ahaziah fell from his upper chamber in Samaria and feared for his life. He sent an envoy to Baal-Zebub, god of Ekron, to discern his fate. Elijah met the envoy on the road and sent a message back to the king from Yahweh: Ahaziah would die. Ahaziah desired to know who sent the message. The messenger said, "He wore a garment of haircloth, with a girdle of leather about his loins" (v8). The king recognized this as a description of Elijah.

2 Kings 1:9–18—Ahaziah ordered the arrest of Elijah. He sent a troop of fifty men to capture him as he rested on the top of a hill. The captain approached Elijah and demanded his surrender. Elijah called down fire from heaven and devoured the company. This happened a second time with another troop. A third troop approached Elijah. This time the captain tried another tactic; he humbly approached Elijah, pleading for his life and the lives of his men. Elijah went with him to see the king. The moral to this story is: Do not command a prophet—always make a request.

2 Kings 2:1–12—Elijah was taken up into heaven in a chariot of fire and in a whirlwind. His faithfulness was rewarded with the ultimate prize: he went to be with God. Enoch and Elijah are the only two people written about in the Bible who did not die. Before Elijah went to heaven, he passed to Elisha a double portion of his spirit.

From the Biblical material, we can easily see the charismatic power of Elijah. He stood up to the evil devices of false prophets and wicked kings. Yet even though the text clearly recognizes the prominence of Elijah, the main character is not Elijah, but God. God overcame Ahab and Jezebel after the murder of Naboth, proclaiming his law to be unconditional and equally applicable to kings as well as subjects. God provided the ravens that fed Elijah and the oil that took care of the widow at Zarephath. God is the maker of prophets, and Elijah was his creation.

Swing Low, Sweet Chariot

Well, I looked over Jordan and what did I see? Comin' for to
    carry me home.
A band of angels comin' after me, Comin' for to carry me home.

Swing low, sweet chariot, Comin' for to carry me home;
Swing low, sweet chariot, Comin' for to carry me home.

Well if you get to heaven before I do, Comin' for to carry me
    home;
Tell all my friends I'm comin' there too, Comin' for to carry
    me home.

Swing low, sweet chariot, Comin' for to carry me home;
Swing low, sweet chariot, Comin' for to carry me home."

—Traditional Spiritual

Life Application

1. What qualities of Elijah impress you? What qualities convict you? What specifically can you change this week to become more like Elijah?

2. Elijah experienced the height of victory as well as the valley of despair. What did God teach him during his valley time? What has God taught you during fearful or discouraging times (currently or in the past)?

3. God provided for Elijah in many miraculous ways. Considering your own walk with God—how would you say he has miraculously provided for you? Take time to thank God for these specific miracles.

4. The study of Elijah in this chapter is a great example of how to study Biblical men and women. Do you study your Bible like this? What can you change to deepen your personal Bible studies?

7

THE CHARISMATIC PROPHETS
Micaiah and Elisha

We now turn our attention to two more charismatic prophets. One is a minor prophet in the sense that little is written about him—Micaiah—but the small amount of material that has been left concerning him is very interesting. The second prophet is one of the greatest prophets of the Old Testament—Elijah. There are many valuable lessons that can be drawn from Elijah's life.

Micaiah

Not much is known of Micaiah Ben Imlah (c. 851 BC). He was one of the charismatic prophets who prophesied during the time of Elijah. Micaiah's story is fascinating. It is the story of a prophet in short-story form. Micaiah's life contains all the elements of Jeremiah's or Isaiah's story, but they are trimmed to one chapter, 1 Kings 22. What do we learn from this "snapshot" of a prophet?

1. A prophet stands for the truth. In 1 Kings 22, Ahab of Israel attempted to form a coalition with Jehoshaphat of Judah to take back Ramoth Gilead from Syria. Jehoshaphat did not wish to go to war at this point, but because his son had married Ahab's daughter, he felt compelled to listen to Ahab. Jehoshaphat suggested that they seek the counsel of God on the matter. Four hundred court prophets ecstatically prophesied before the two kings as they sat enthroned in their royal garb. Jehoshaphat recognized that he was listening to Ahab's "yes" men, and he requested another prophet. Ahab protested, knowing that the only voice left was that of the true prophet, Micaiah. The king scoffed, "'I hate him, for he never prophesies good concerning me, but evil'" (v8). This was because Micaiah prophesied only the truth.

Micaiah was forced to have an audience with Ahab and Jehoshaphat. Even as he approached the palace, the royal messenger reminded Micaiah that the court prophets spoke favorably of the military campaign. Micaiah responded, "As Yahweh lives, what Yahweh says to me, that will I speak" (v14). Micaiah was only interested in delivering God's message, not in pleasing the king.

Micaiah's first statement to Ahab was a sarcastic mimic of the court prophets, "'Go up and triumph'" (v15). Without smiling, Ahab answered, "Speak to me nothing but the truth" (v16). Micaiah told Ahab that the battle would mean his death. Ahab looked over to Jehoshaphat and sulked, "Did I not tell you that he would not prophesy good concerning me, but evil?" (v18).

The concern of all the prophets was to speak the true message of God. If this message pleased or displeased the hearer, it did not concern the prophets. They had to speak the Word that God gave them.

2. *A prophet dreams God's dreams.* When Ahab raised his protest against Micaiah's message, he was not prepared for Micaiah's response. Micaiah had seen the heavenly council of God, leaving us a description of this celestial scene in 1 Kings 22:19–23. This is one of the most intriguing passages in the Bible. Micaiah saw God sitting on a throne, with the heavenly host to his right and left. God was holding an advisory hearing on what should be done to King Ahab. God was looking for someone to entice Ahab so he would fall. A spirit stepped forward (if spirits step) to volunteer. He said he would approach Ahab as "a lying spirit in the mouth of all his prophets." God replied, "You are to entice him, and you shall succeed; go forth and do so" (v22).

How are we to understand this scene? Is God allowing a lie to take down Ahab—even sanctioning it to be so? We know that God uses unjust instruments to carry out his judgment on people (for example, Nebuchadnezzar against Jerusalem), but would he allow one of *his* spirits to propagate a lie in order to bring justice? Can God accept a lie under any condition? These are a few of the questions raised by this passage. They are not easy questions. We all must struggle for the answers.

A verse that seems related to this passage is found in 2 Thessalonians 2:11–12:

> For this reason God sends them a powerful delusion so that they will believe the lie and so that all will be condemned who have not believed the truth but have delighted in wickedness.

Perhaps we are to understand these passages as simply expressing the sovereignty of God. God controls this world and allows good and evil to exist. Because God allows this to be so, we are given a choice between good and evil. Ahab was drawn to evil because he believed a lie. God allowed that lie to exist to give Ahab the chance to choose right from wrong. God still allows that choice for all of us today.

Certainly the only reason this story survived and was included in the canon is because it was a real vision recorded by a real prophet. Micaiah saw something no one else had ever seen. How could the prophets do and say what they did? They had seen God.

3. A prophet suffers many trials. The role of the prophet was not for the fainthearted, weak or faithless. Although some prophets may have started with these qualities in their lives, God transformed them into courageous men and women. The prophets faced persecution. Micaiah had to suspect how Ahab would react to his message. Ahab was a violent tyrant. To him, murder was a pastime. Yet Micaiah did not back down.

After Micaiah prophesied to Ahab, Zedekiah, one of the court prophets, slapped him in the face. Micaiah looked at Zedekiah and basically said, "Just wait, someday you'll get what's coming to you." Then Ahab placed Micaiah under arrest. He put Micaiah in maximum security under the eye of his own son and ordered, "'Feed him with scant fare of bread and water" (v27).

We do not know what Ahab ultimately did with Micaiah. The details are not important. The same story is told over and over again in the lives of the prophets. The prophet suffered. He suffered for doing right. He suffered for speaking a message that was true. He suffered for seeing things that few mortal men have ever seen. He suffered because God called him.

Elisha

Elisha is first mentioned in the Scriptures as being the successor to Elijah. He followed Elijah as a charismatic prophet and even inherited a double portion of Elijah's charisma. What made Elisha a great prophet? Why is he such a heroic Biblical figure? I hope that as you look at the Biblical text on the life of Elisha, you will gain an understanding of his life. I hope that what I have gleaned from the Scriptures will help you in your Bible study.

1 Kings 19:19–21—Elijah called Elisha to follow his role as a prophet. Elisha was a farmer; he was an ordinary person with an ordinary job. When he received his call, he killed his oxen and prepared them for roasting. He took the yoke, which was used for plowing, and chopped it into firewood. By roasting his oxen, he was saying goodbye to his old life. He was ready to be a prophet. He had closed all exits.

Elisha's call sets the tone for the prophetic call throughout Israel's history. When God called the prophets, they had to decide to leave behind their families, vocations and personal desires to follow a higher purpose—God's calling.

2 Kings 2:1–14—Elisha followed Elijah to the place where God would receive him into heaven. When Elijah asked Elisha to stop, Elisha begged to continue. When Elijah asked him to request anything, Elisha requested a double portion of Elijah's spirit. Elisha was a loyal disciple to Elijah. He desired to be like him and went the extra mile to be with him. Because of his loyalty, he received Elijah's blessing.

2 Kings 2:15–22—A community of prophets gathered around the charismatic leadership of Elisha. They became known as the sons of the prophets, and they set up a community near a peaceful city. Elisha demonstrated God's power to care for his people by throwing salt into bitter water and making it pure.

2 Kings 2:23–25—Some small boys mocked Elisha, calling him "baldhead." He responded by causing two she-bears to leave the woods and kill forty-two of the boys. Not many writers would have included this as a story to venerate a prophet. In our human wisdom we might even have left this story out of the canon. But everything in the Bible is there for a purpose, even though that purpose might elude our understanding.[1] Whatever this passage might teach, one thing is certain—I doubt that anyone ever called Elijah a "baldhead" again. To insult a prophet of God is to insult God.[2]

2 Kings 3:1–27—Elisha predicted victory for Jehoram. Jehoram, the son of Ahab, reigned over Israel at the death of his brother, Ahaziah. Jehoram joined forces with Jehoshaphat, king of Judah, and the vassal king of Edom to fight against Mesha, king of Moab. On their march through Edom to Moab a drought caught the army. They were left without water as they stared into the face of battle. Jehoshaphat requested a prophet to determine the outcome of their dire situation. Elisha arrived and called for a minstrel upon whose playing the power of Yahweh came to Elisha. He prophesied that not only would water come, but also that Israel would win a victory over Moab. They did win a victory so decisive that Mesha's only recourse to stop Israel was to sacrifice his oldest son. This frightened Israel into retreat.

2 Kings 4:1–7—Elisha allowed a prophet's widow to pay her debts by miraculously filling vessels with oil. This enabled her to keep her sons from being claimed into child slavery. The widow trusted God, and he came through for her.

2 Kings 4:8–37—A Shunammite woman showed kindness to Elisha by building him a room upon the roof of her house. In return, Elisha informed her that though she was childless, she would bear a son. One day, while the promised son was in the fields with his father, he had a seizure and died. The Shunammite woman rode out to find Elisha. After she informed Elisha of her loss, Elisha sent his servant back to the boy with his staff. The servant was ineffective, and the boy remained dead. Elisha prayed over the boy and laid on top of him, and the boy came back to life. In the midst of darkness, the Shunammite woman trusted, and God came through.

---

[1] Richard Nelson, an OT professor, suggests that this story was told as a bogeyman story—be good or Elisha will get you. Richard Nelson, *First and Second Kings* (Louisville, Kentucky: John Knox Press, 1987) 157.

[2] *The New Oxford Annotated Bible* adds this quip in its notes: "Mt. 19:13 –15, Mk. 10:13 –16, Lk. 18:15 –17 provide a better guide to Biblical teaching on how to treat children." *The New Oxford Annotated Bible with the Apocrypha*, ed. by Herbert G. May and Bruce M. Metzger (New York: Oxford University Press, 1977) 456.

2 *Kings* 4:38–41—During a famine in Gilgal, a member of Elisha's community accidentally placed poisonous herbs into a pot of soup for the community. Elisha relieved the situation by placing meal in the pot, making the venomous brew edible. Once again God provided for his people.

2 *Kings* 4:42–44—A man from Baal Shalishah brought Elisha twenty loaves of barley bread from his firstfruits. Elisha asked his servant to give the loaves to the hundred men who were with Elisha. The man protested that the bread would not be adequate to feed one hundred men. Elisha responded that not only would it be adequate, but there would be leftovers. Elisha's prediction proved true.

2 *Kings* 5:1–19—Elisha told Naaman, a commander of the Syrian army, how to be cleansed of leprosy. Naaman was to dip seven times in the Jordan River. Although Naaman protested at first, he humbled himself and became obedient. He was cleansed. When non-Hebrews believed and trusted in God, he made his power available to them.

2 *Kings* 5:20–27—Elisha's servant, Gehazi, ran after Naaman to con him out of the gifts he offered Elisha. Elisha's spirit ran alongside of Naaman, informing him of Gehazi's actions. Gehazi was cursed by Elisha. He and his descendants would suffer with leprosy. Gehazi was disloyal to the prophet and to God. He was punished for his insubordinate behavior.

2 *Kings* 6:1–7—Elisha's community moved near the Jordan. As the men chopped trees for building material, the head of one of the axes flew off into the water. The man wielding the ax was upset because he had borrowed it. Elisha caused it to float, and it was retrieved.

2 *Kings* 6:8–23—Elisha had the ability to know the mind of the king of Syria even ten miles away. The king sent a strong force to seize Elisha, so the espionage would end. The Syrians surrounded Elisha, but he was not afraid. He enabled his servant, who was afraid, to see God's army of horses and fiery chariots waiting to stop the Syrians. God never wants his people to be afraid. Elisha

caused the army to go blind, and then led the captives before the king of Israel in Samaria. Elisha trusted and God delivered.

2 Kings 6:24–7:20—Ben-Hadad, king of Syria, besieged Samaria until a famine engulfed the city. The famine was so severe that two women agreed to trade off eating their children to stay alive. One woman boiled her child, and they satisfied their hunger. The second woman reneged on the agreement. When the king heard the story, he grieved. He blamed Elisha for the city's condition because Elisha was a representative of God. Elisha did not accept the blame, but he informed the king that the famine would end and Samaria would prosper again. A gatekeeper of the king scoffed at Elisha for his optimism. Elisha predicted his death for his pessimism. Later in the story, the gatekeeper died.

Four lepers decided to investigate the Syrian camp, thinking to themselves, "If they kill us, then our condition has not changed, because we are as good as dead in this famine." Their reasoning proved to be a blessing. God had sent the Syrian army scurrying back home without Israel's knowledge. The lepers informed the king of the situation, but he was skeptical, suspecting a trap. The lepers' word proved to be true, and Samaria was spared.

2 Kings 8:1–6—Elisha warned the Shunammite woman about a seven-year famine, which would decimate the land. She left and went to Philistia for seven years. Upon returning to her home, she entreated the king to return her house and her property, which she had left behind. By Hebrew law, the property was still hers. The king was informed that this woman was a friend of Elisha. He allowed her the land because of Elisha. She trusted the prophet and placed her life and her property in his hands. God blessed her trust.

2 Kings 8:7–15—Elisha predicted the death of Ben-Hadad of Damascus and the rise of his son Hazael to power. Elisha wept because he knew the pain that Damascus would cause Israel. Elisha was a man of love and compassion.

2 Kings 9:1–37—Elisha sent a prophet to anoint Jehu as the next king of Israel. Jehu's reign marked the end of the dynasty of Omri. By anointing Hazael of Damascus and Jehu of Israel, Elisha completed two of the three prophecies made to Elijah on Mount Horeb in 1 Kings 19. God's word always proves to be true.

2 Kings 13:14–19—King Joash sought counsel from Elisha, who was on his deathbed, as to Israel's fate with regard to the Syrians. Elisha helped him shoot arrows out of the east window to signify victory over the Syrians. He asked the king to strike the ground with his arrows. Joash struck the ground three times. Elisha grew angry, exclaiming,

> "You should have struck five or six times, thus you
> would have struck down Syria until you had made an
> end of it, but now you will strike down Syria only three
> times."

Israel paid for Joash's tentativeness.

2 Kings 13:20–21—Elisha died and was buried. That spring, another man died. A marauding band from Moab was seen, and so his body was thrown into Elisha's grave. When his body touched Elisha's bones, he came back to life. Elisha's power lived on, even after his death.

Learning from Elisha's character

1. Elisha was a great learner and a great teacher. Although ideas about discipling are generally thought of as NT concepts, they can readily be seen in Elisha's life because the principle of making disciples has its roots in the Old Testament. Samuel had a band or procession of prophets gathered around him. This idea of a community of disciples is also seen in the life of Isaiah (see Isaiah 8). Elisha perpetuated this tradition of gathering around him a school of prophets. They regarded Elisha as their master and honored him as their father.

Elisha learned the concept by placing himself at Elijah's feet. He learned how to disciple by being a disciple. He responded to Elijah's call to prophesy and followed Elijah in his ministry. At the end of Elijah's life, Elisha desired to be just like Elijah and wanted to take his own ministry higher than his predecessor's.

When Elijah passed his mantle to Elisha, men saw Elisha as their mentor. Elisha assembled these men to train them so that Yahwism would not die in the land. Gehard von Rad, a great German OT scholar, has written:

In the long run, these men were the parents of that stupendous radicalization of Yahwism and its law which we find in the later prophets. They laid the foundations of that mysterious social and economic detachment and that disregard for the consideration of state policies, which were the unquestioned preconditions for the rest of the later prophetic movement.[3]

Unlike other great leaders through the centuries, Elisha invested himself into others so that his work would not die with him. Elisha believed in making disciples.

2. *Elisha allowed God to work powerfully through him.* He performed powerful miracles. As Elisha received a double portion of Elijah's spirit, he also received a double portion of Elijah's mighty works. Elisha came into the land like a hurricane, and his power never dimmed. Elisha made iron float, purified a polluted spring of water, struck an enemy army with blindness, healed a leper and brought the dead back to life. God's power was evident in Elisha's life and was confirmed by his mighty works. These deeds emphasized the righteousness of this great prophet of God.

3. *Elisha influenced people, both great and small.* The ultimate test of leadership is being able to motivate people. A true leader must move people on all societal levels, from the prince to the pauper. Moses moved a whole nation to freedom. Jesus moved all of history by his life. Elisha moved people as well.

People came from great distances to sit at Elisha's feet and to receive counsel from him. He helped both widows and kings. He was responsible for the fall of Omri's dynasty, the most wicked dynasty to rule in Israel. Elisha reformed the political, social and religious environment of his day. When a battalion of the army of Aram came to capture him, he struck them blind and took them to the city of Samaria, where they were captured. Elisha met the test of great leadership—he inspired people.

4. *Elisha demonstrated tireless compassion for the individual.* When Elisha discovered that a widow of a former member of his prophetic company was in trouble with her creditors, he gave her oil, filling every vessel she and her sons could find. Elisha

promised a Shunammite woman, who was without child, that she would have a son. The prophecy was fulfilled, and she had a child. One day the boy died. The woman asked Elisha to restore her son, and he complied with her wish. Later, Elisha again saved this woman and her son by sending them to the land of Palestine while there was a seven-year famine in Israel. A commander of the army of Aram came to Elisha to be cleansed of leprosy. Elisha healed the foreign dignitary, choosing to receive no compensation for his effort. Elisha was not concerned with money; his concern was for the individual.

Elisha's care for the individual foreshadows Jesus' ministry. No one has ever cared for the individual like Jesus of Nazareth. When we read the Gospels in a cursory fashion, it seems as if Jesus spent most of his time talking to the multitudes and moving among the crowds. But upon closer inspection, the bulk of the ministry of Jesus was spent with individuals and small groups. Even when he was among the crowds, he took time to recognize the needs of the one amongst thousands. This was true in the case of the woman with an issue of blood, and for Zacchaeus and others whom Jesus touched in passing. Jesus came to save the whole world, but he came to save it one by one. He cared for the individual more radically than anyone who has ever lived.

Elisha powerfully exemplifies the charismatic prophet of Israel. Little is known of what he taught, his view of God or his ethics. What is known of him is seen in his lifestyle and his mighty works. He fought against the religious syncretism of Israel and for the patriarchal concepts of Yahweh. He became a pattern for the prophets who were to follow—those of the classical period of prophecy.

Life Application

1. Micaiah suffered for speaking God's truth. Has this ever happened to you? How did you handle it? How has studying the prophets helped you in this area?

2. What are some things or people you have left in order to follow Jesus? How do you feel about this decision? How has God blessed this sacrifice?

3. There are many parallels between the lives of Elijah and Elisha and the life of Jesus. What are some similarities that you have noticed in your readings?

4. Elisha was a great student to Elijah. How are your discipling relationships? Do you have someone you are teaching/training to be like Jesus? Do you have someone in your life to teach and train you? If not, what can you do to change this?

8

CLASSICAL PROPHETS AND THE ULTIMATE PROPHET

It was twenty years ago today
Sergeant Pepper taught the band to play

—John Lennon and Paul McCartney

Every movement of humanity has a period that people point to and call a classical period. The classic period of rock was introduced by four kids from Liverpool, England. The Beatles arrived in the United States in the mid-sixties and took the country by storm. The Establishment did not know what to do with them. The press did not know how to handle their playful behavior. But the guys knew exactly what to do—they took music to a totally new dimension! In the midst of the psychedelic era, the Beatles wove a tapestry of sound created by the noises of a restless generation and recorded it for history to savor. With the song writing team of Lennon and McCartney, and the production genius of George Martin, the Beatles produced hit after hit. No one has accomplished as much before or since. The Beatles are the essence of rock and roll.

The Classical Period of Prophecy

Israel's greatest time of prophetic activity, the classical period, occurred between 750 and 550 BC. As lighthouses guide erring ships to safety, so the prophets called a nation on the verge of shipwreck back to Yahweh. Only Jesus has proclaimed the word of God more clearly. These men and women were willing to give up homes, prestige, comfort and security to declare Yahweh's message. They essentially placed their necks on the chopping block because of their love for God.

During the years of the divided monarchy, the prophetic class became an accepted and honored part of Israelite society. They were given a place at the king's court and in the religious cultus. Yet, their acceptance became their hazard. With acceptance came the temptation for false prophets to arise and speak whatever the people wanted to hear. This was especially true of court prophets, who desired to please the king and keep him happy. He was received into the status quo of Israelite life. And when the prophet became comfortable, the word of the Lord grew silent.

At this point, lightning flashed onto the scene. The classical prophets arose to lift up the word of Yahweh and to declare it to the people with uncompromising clarity. First, there was Amos. This shepherd delivered a message of social reform, with biting criticism, to the upper echelon of society. He led the way for the prophets who spoke up against the false prophets of their day. The classical prophets followed in the vein of Moses, Samuel, Elijah and Elisha, demanding obedience and reverence for God's law as revealed in the Torah.

Then think of the great loss to our understanding of the remnant if Isaiah had not lived. How would we understand God's continual, consistent love without Hosea? What if Jeremiah had not dictated his oracles to Baruch? The classical prophets recorded the message of God's revelation, and it inspires us. They left us a rich memory that cannot be erased.

Volumes two and three of this work will consider the writings of the prophets of the classical period. Each written prophet from this period will be studied in detail. Because we have their writings, the classical prophets influence our understanding of prophecy more than any of the previously mentioned prophets. Their written legacy has been studied, written about and preached from for centuries.

The Written Prophets

The Decline and Fall of Samaria at the Hand of the Assyrians

Book	Meaning	Date (BC)	Theme of Book
Amos	*burden bearer*	786–742 Israel	Samaria must fall because of her sins
Jonah	*dove*	780–740 Nineveh	Universality of God's love
Hosea	*salvation*	745–715 Israel	Condemnation for idolatry and God's continuing love
Micah	*who is like Yahweh?*	740–710 Judah	Obey God from a true and trusting heart
Isaiah	*Yahweh is salvation*	742–698 Judah	Salvation is God's gift

The Decline and Fall of Judah at the Hands of the Babylonians

Book	Meaning	Date (BC)	Theme of Book
Zephaniah	*hidden by Yahweh*	621 Judah	The day of the Lord
Nahum	*consolation, relief, comfort*	615–612 Judah	Destruction of Nineveh
Habakkuk	*embrace*	605 Judah	God will rule; the righteous shall live by faith
Jeremiah	*God establishes*	626–562 Judah	Judah will fall because of her sins

Figure 1—*continued on next page*

Jesus

> Jesus Christ, superstar.
> Do you think you're who
> They say you are?
>
> —Tim Rice, songwriter

No one has inspired more singing or poetry than Jesus. Elijah spoke prophecies. Isaiah and Jeremiah wrote prophecies. But no one has inspired more prophecy to be spoken or more prophecy

The Written Prophets—*continued*

The Restoration Permitted by Persia

Book	Meaning	Date (BC)	Theme of Book
Daniel	*God has judged*	605–530 The exiles	Prophecy of God's ultimate triumph
Ezekiel	*God strengthens*	592–570 The exiles	The sure destruction of Jerusalem and the reestablishment of Israel
Haggai	*the festive one*	536 Israel	Revive true worship; rebuild the temple
Zechariah	*he whom God remembers*	520–516 Israel	Rebuke for complacency and hypocrisy
Malachi	*my messenger*	445–432 Israel	Rebuke for complacency and hypocrisy
Prophets of Indefinite Date			
Joel	*Yahweh is God*	Judah	Repent—the day of the Lord is at hand
Obadiah	*the servant of Yahweh*	Judah	Destruction of Edom

Figure 1—*continued*

to be written than Jesus. The world of professional sports may have its superstars: in baseball, there was only one Babe Ruth. In football, only one Walter Payton. In basketball, only one Michael Jordan. In hockey, only one Wayne Gretzky. But in the real-life world of prophets and kings, there was and is only one Jesus of Nazareth.

Jesus was superior to all the other prophets. His superiority is illustrated in the story of the transfiguration (Matthew 17:1–8, Mark 9:2–8, Luke 9:28–36). Moses, the great giver of the law, and Elijah, the greatest of the prophets, appeared with Jesus on the Mount of Olives. Peter, James and John recognized the greatness of these two figures and desired to build booths to honor them. A voice came out of heaven, pronouncing who really deserved honor:

"This is my beloved Son, with whom I am well pleased" (Matthew 17:5). God demonstrated that Jesus was greater than the law or the prophets.

Through the centuries humanity has paid homage to the prophets of Israel. We have lauded their commitment and praised their conviction. We have been challenged by their upward call to a simple, spiritual life. Through the ages the prophets of Israel have paid homage to one who is superior to them in every way: Jesus of Nazareth.

Jesus—The Ultimate Prophetic Ministry

The way in which Jesus ministered to people was prophetic. He was different from the rabbis of his day. He went to the people instead of waiting for the people to come to him. He loved the stingy, wealthy tax collector and the poor, lost beggar. No one escaped the reach of his love. He touched the leper and hugged the prostitute. He spoke to Samaritans and praised the faith of the Gentiles. Jesus broke the social and religious norms of his day. He went further than any prophet before him had gone.

Luke 7 gives us insight into Jesus' ministry through the eyes of John the Baptist. John the Baptist began to doubt if Jesus was the true Messiah sent from God. He sent some of his followers to question Jesus to see if he was the one they were anticipating. Jesus sent them back to John, saying:

> "Go and tell John what you have seen and heard: the blind receive their sight, the lame walk, lepers are cleansed, and the deaf hear, the dead are raised up, the poor have good news preached to them. And blessed is he who takes no offense at me." (Luke 7:22 –23)

The ministry of Jesus was radically different from other messianic figures. His life was filled with the good works that he did, demonstrating that he was the true Messiah.

Even though Jesus continually helped people, his ministry still met with much opposition. Some said he was possessed by a demon (Mark 3:22). His own family thought he was out of his mind (Mark 3). The hypocritical religious leaders of his day sought to destroy him (Luke 19:47). Political enemies joined forces to destroy him (Mark 3:6). Yet, with all this opposition, he never stopped doing good. No amount of criticism could paralyze him. Satan himself could not stop the ministry of Jesus. His ministry was prophetic because it followed in the traditions of the OT prophets. It was prophetic because it called everyone around him to live by a higher standard—God's standard.

Jesus—The Ultimate Prophetic Teaching

No one who has ever walked the earth taught as powerfully and effectively as did Jesus of Nazareth. His parables were wonderfully descriptive. His discourses on God inspired people to new heights of spirituality. His explanation of the law demonstrated insight beyond that of any other man. His was a message of truth taught with an unparalleled passion.

The greatest example of the superiority of Jesus' teaching is the Sermon on the Mount (Matthew 5–7). Here Jesus established the ethic of his new community. His people were to be different from the world. In fact, they were to be a light to the world. They were to season the world with the message of love, as salt seasons meat. They were to live by a law written on the heart. To them, sin was not just an outward act, but thoughts and attitudes could also be sinful. The community of Jesus was called out of the world to be a city set upon a hill—different and unique from all the cities around it.

After Jesus finished his Sermon on the Mount, Matthew gave us another insight into why Jesus' teaching was unique: people noticed that Jesus taught with authority (Matthew 7:28–29). In other words Jesus knew he was sent from God and that the message he taught was the word of God. He had radical confidence because he spoke the word of God; this confidence impressed people. His words were challenging, but they were truthful. His words came from his heart, he taught them with passion.

Jesus was a bottom-line kind of man. I like that about him. I like that he did not beat around the bush—he spoke directly about the issue at hand. When Jesus saw Zacchaeus, the corrupt tax collector, up in a tree, he basically said, "Come down from there and fix me some dinner." When Peter tempted Jesus to give up the cross, Jesus essentially responded, "Get away from me, Satan. I will not tolerate your lack of faith." When the rich young ruler questioned Jesus about eternal life, Jesus stopped the man in mid-sentence, telling him what he needed to hear (in modern vernacular): "You must give up everything you own—your house and your summer cottage, your Mercedes and your Jaguar, your salary and your pension—and follow me."

Jesus told people what they needed to hear, not just what they wanted to hear. This is one reason why his teaching was superior to that of the rabbis. He taught with confidence and authority. He said exactly what needed to be said, no matter how hard it was to say, just like the prophets of old. Yes, his was the ultimate prophetic teaching.

Jesus—The Ultimate Prophetic Symbol

Many of the OT prophets performed radical acts to get their message across to the people. Ezekiel laid on his side for more than a year as a prophetic symbol to the Jews in exile. Isaiah walked around barefoot and naked for more than three years to demonstrate what the Babylonians would do to their enemies. Hosea married a prostitute so that he could understand the love of God for Israel. These were all wild, radical prophetic acts. But none of these surpasses the extreme action of Jesus as he died on the cross for the sins of humanity. Jesus performed the ultimate act of sacrifice.

Paul understood the death of Jesus as being a demonstration of God's love for humanity. In Romans 5:6–8 he wrote,

> While we were still weak, at the right time Christ died for the ungodly. Why, one will hardly die for a right-eous man—though perhaps for a good man one will dare even to die. But God shows his love for us in that while we were yet sinners Christ died for us.

We might die for someone we love and adore, but Christ died for those who were unlovable and depraved. Paul saw the death of Jesus on the cross as the greatest symbol of God's love for humanity.

Peter understood the crucifixion as a powerful motivating symbol for righteousness. Once we understand the nature of the sacrifice of Jesus on the cross and the fact that our sins put him there, we strive to live without sin. Concerning Jesus, the apostle Peter states,

> When he was reviled, he did not revile in return; when he suffered, he did not threaten; but he trusted to him who judges justly. He himself bore our sins in his body on the tree, that we might die to sin and live to righteousness. By his wounds you have been healed. For you were straying like sheep, but have now returned to the Shepherd and Guardian of your souls. (1 Peter 2:23 –25)

Jesus bore the marks of the cross upon his body for our sins. When we sin, it is as though we crucify him all over again; therefore, we should avoid sin. Peter saw the cross as a prophetic symbol, motivating us to stay away from sin.

Jesus' crucifixion was the ultimate prophetic symbol. But Jesus' death was much more than a symbol. It was the action needed to pay the price for our sins. His death was the most meaningful act of sacrifice to ever be performed. Jesus was suspended on a cross between heaven and earth in order that he might close the gap between heaven and earth. The centurion standing near the cross watched this selfless act of love and reached the only possible conclusion, "'Surely this man was the Son of God!'" (Matthew 27:54, Mark 15:39, Luke 23:47 NIV). Only the Son of God could provide this greatest of all prophetic symbols.

The lives of many great prophets are recorded in Scripture, but the ultimate prophet was Jesus of Nazareth. No one ever poured himself out in the ministry the way Jesus did. His was the ultimate prophetic ministry. No one ever taught the way he did—with authority and truth. His was the ultimate prophetic teaching. No one ever used prophetic symbols the way he did. His death on the cross was the ultimate prophetic symbol. Jesus was superior to all the other prophets.

In history there have been many great composers. But there will be only one Wolfgang Amadeus Mozart. In literature there will be many great authors, but there will be only one William Shakespeare. In art there have been many great artists, but there will be only one Michelangelo Buonarroti. In God's history with humanity there have been many great prophets, but there will be only one Jesus of Nazareth, the superstar of prophets.

When I was hungry, you gave me to eat.
When I was thirsty, you gave me to drink.
Whatsoever you do to the least of my brethren
That you do unto me.
Now enter the house of my Father.

When I was weary, you helped me find rest.
When I was anxious, you calmed all my fears.
When I was homeless, you opened your doors.
When I was naked, you gave me your coat.
When I was little, you taught me to read.
When I was lonely, you gave me your love.
When in a prison, you came to my cell.
When on a sick bed, you cared for my needs.
In a strange country, you made me at home.
Seeking employment, you found me a job.
Hurt in a battle, you bound up my wounds.
Searching for kindness, you held out your hand.

When I was Negro, or Chinese, or white,
And mocked and insulted, you carried my cross.

When I was aged, you bothered to smile.
When I was restless, you listened and cared.
You saw me covered with spittle and blood.
You knew my features, though grimy with sweat.
When I was laughed at, you stood by my side.
When I was happy, you shared in my joy.

—Mother Teresa of Calcutta

Life Application

1. What impresses you the most about Jesus? In what ways has he prophesied to your heart?
2. Jesus' love was revolutionary, and he calls us to imitate him. How have you expressed Jesus' love this past week to others? How can you express his love next week?
3. Jesus' crucifixion was the ultimate prophetic symbol. Have you been reflecting on and been motivated by the cross? What can you do to draw closer to the cross?

PART IV

A HISTORICAL SURVEY OF THE PROPHETIC PERIOD

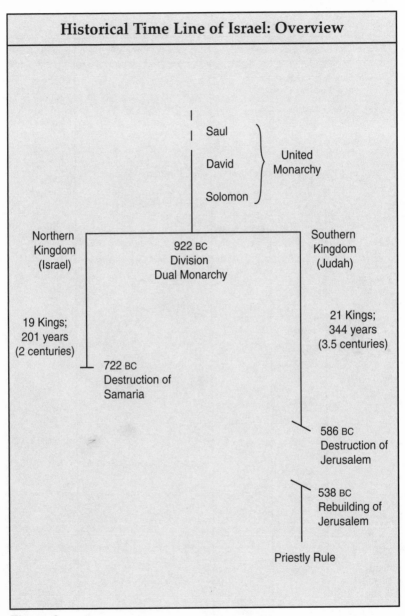

Historical Time Line of Israel: Overview

Saul

David

Solomon

United Monarchy

Northern Kingdom (Israel)

922 BC Division Dual Monarchy

Southern Kingdom (Judah)

19 Kings; 201 years (2 centuries)

21 Kings; 344 years (3.5 centuries)

722 BC Destruction of Samaria

586 BC Destruction of Jerusalem

538 BC Rebuilding of Jerusalem

Priestly Rule

Figure 2

Historical Time Line of Israel

Events Occuring Around Palestine			Dominant Foreign Powers	Biblical Book
c. 1000 David becomes King in Jerusalem				1 Samuel
				2 Samuel
c. 965 Solomon becomes King over Israel				1 Chronicles
c. 931 Division of Hebrew Kingdom				
	Kings of Israel and Judah		**Kings of Assyria**	1 Kings
	Israel	**Judah**		2 Chronicles
	931-910 Jeroboam I	931-913 Rehoboam	934-912 Ashur-dan II	
924 Shishak invades Palestine				
		913-911 Abijah		
	910-909 Nadab	911-870 Asa	911-891 Adad-nirari II	
	909-886 Baasha			
			890-884 Tukulti-Ninurta II	
	886-885 Elah			
	885 Zimri			
	885-874 Omri		883-859 Ashurnasirpal II	
	874-853 Ahab	870-848 Jehoshaphat		
853 Ahab defeated by Shalmaneser III at Qarqar	853-852 Ahaziah		858-824 Shalmaneser III	
	852-841 Joram	848-841 Jehoram		2 Kings

Figure 3—*continued on next page*

Historical Time Line of Israel—*continued*

Events Occuring Around Palestine			Dominant Foreign Powers	Biblical Book
	Israel	**Judah**		
841-Jehu pays tribute to Shalmaneser III	841-814 Jehu	841 Ahaziah 841-835 Athaliah 835-796 Jehoash/ Joash		
			823-811 Shamshi-Adad V	
	814-798 Jehoahaz		810-783 Adad-nirari III	
	798-782 Joash/ Jehoash	796-767 Amaziah		
	782-753 Jeroboam II		782-773 Shalmaneser IV 772-755 Ashur-dan III	
		767-740 Uzziah/ Azariah		Amos Jonah
			754-745 Ashur-irari V	Hosea
	753-752 Zechariah			
	752 Shallum			
	752-742 Menahem			
	742-740 Pekahiah		744-727 Tiglath-Pileser III	Isaiah
738-Menahem's tribute to Tiglath-Pileser III	752-732 Pekah	740-732 Jotham		
734-Ahaz's tribute to Tiglath-Pileser III				
732-Tiglath-Pileser III places Hoshea on throne	732-723 Hoshea	732-716 Ahaz/ Jehoahaz I		
722-Fall of Samaria			726-722 Shalmaneser V	Micah
			721-705 Sargon II	

Figure 3—*continued*

Historical Time Line of Israel—*continued*

Events Occuring Around Palestine		Dominant Foreign Powers	Biblical Book
	Judah		
	716-687 Hezekiah		
712-Sargon II's campaign to Ashdod			
		704-681 Sennacherib	
701-Lachish attacked by Sennacherib			
	687-643 Manasseh	680-669 Esarhaddon	
670-Manasseh pays tribute to Esarhadden	643-641 Amon	668-627 Ashurbanipal	
	641-609 Josiah	626-624? Ashur-etel-ilani Sin-shumu-lishir	Jeremiah
612-Fall of Nineveh		612 Sin-sharra-ishkun	Zephaniah
609-Josiah slain by Nechoh II of Egypt	609 Jehoahaz II	611-609 Ashur-uballit II	
		CHALDEAN DYNASTY	Nahum
	609-598 Jehoiakim	625-605 Nabopolassar 605-562 Nebuchadnezzar II	Habakkuk
597-Nebuchadnezzar II conquers Jerusalem; Jehoiachin deported to Babylon	598-597 Jehoiachin 597-586 Zedekiah		Daniel
587-Fall of Jerusalem and beginning of exile			Obadiah(?) Ezekiel
561-Release of Jehoiachin 559-Cyrus becomes King of Persia		561-560 Evil-Merodach 559-556 Neriglissar 556 Labashi-Markuk 555-539 Nabonidus	
545-Fall of Sardis 539-Fall of Babylon 530-Cambyses becomes King of Persia 525-Cambyses takes Egypt			Haggai

Figure 3—*continued*

Historical Time Line of Israel—*continued*

Events Occuring Around Palestine	Dominant Foreign Powers	Biblical Book
522 Darius I King of Persia		Zechariah
c. 520 Rebuilding of temple at Jerusalem		
490 First Persian Invasion of Greece; Battle of Marathon 486 Xerxes I King of Persia		

480 Second Persian invasion
    of Greece;
    Battles of Thermopylae,
    Salamis and Plataea (479)
		(Esther)

464 Artaxerxes I King of Persia;
    (?)Ezra reads the Law in
    Jerusalem;
    Nehemiah rebuilds the walls of
    Jerusalem
		Nehemiah
		Malachi

423 Darius II King of Persia		
411-410 Jewish temple at Elephantine destroyed		Ezra

404 Artaxerxes II King of Persia;
    Egypt rebels against Persia;
    (?)Ezra reads the Law in
    Jerusalem
		Joel
		Obadiah(?)
		Ruth

359 Artaxerxes III King of Persia		
336 Alexander the Great Darius III King of Persia		
332 Alexander the Great destroys the Persian Empire		
323 Beginning of Rule of Seleucids; Death of Alexander the Great		

Figure 3—*continued*

9

THE NORTHERN KINGDOM

To fully understand the writings of the prophets, we must have a working knowledge of their historical environs. The prophets were more interested in events of their own day than in the future. Therefore, it is important to know the times and conditions of the society in which they lived.

The separate history of Israel and Judah begins with the division of the monarchy of Israel and continues through the fall of Judah at the hand of Nebuchadnezzar of Babylon. In the following three chapters, the kings of Israel and Judah are listed in chronological order and a brief sketch is given about each of the kings. This material corresponds with the events described in 1 Kings 11 through 2 Kings. Provided is information from the Biblical text and details from Israelite history. This section should in no way serve as a substitute for reading the Biblical text, and is not necessarily intended to be read all at once. It serves more as a reference for any unknown king who may be encountered while studying the prophets. One can refer back to these chapters to get a summary of the life of the kings of Israel and Judah.

Precursor to Division
Solomon (965–922 BC) 1 Kings 11

The kingdom of Israel reached its apex under the leadership David's son, Solomon, who brought fame and fortune to the capital, Jerusalem. Solomon built the royal palace and the temple of Yahweh, which throughout Israelite history were unequalled in their grandeur. Solomon accomplished feats that David could not. But one essential quality separated David and Solomon—heart.

"And his [Solomon's] heart was not wholly true to the Lord his God, as was the heart of David his father" (1 Kings 11:4). Solomon's heart had a dark side to it, which is described in 1 Kings 11. Solomon's seven hundred wives and three hundred concubines turned his heart away from God. To please his wives, he promoted the worship of idols on the mountains east of Jerusalem. Because Solomon departed from God, God departed from Solomon. Yahweh informed Solomon that he would tear the kingdom away from him, giving ten tribes to one of his servants (Jeroboam), while allowing another tribe to stay in his house because of God's affection for David and Jerusalem. (One other tribe, Levi, received no allotment of land.) These events did not unfold in Solomon's lifetime, but they did occur later in history.

The Northern Kingdom of Israel/Samaria
Jeroboam I (931–910 BC) 1 Kings 11–14; 2 Chronicles 10

The prophet Ahijah of Shiloh tore his mantle into twelve pieces and gave ten of these to Jeroboam (1 Kings 11:29–39). This was a symbol of the division of the united monarchy of David and Solomon coming to an end. This action brought the wrath of Solomon upon Jeroboam, who then fled to Egypt and sought safety from Shishak, king of Egypt. Shishak (935–914 BC) was the founder of the twenty-second dynasty in Egypt. For the first time in three centuries, since the death of Merneptah (the ruler after Rameses II) in 1211 BC, Egypt once again had an opportunity to flex her muscles in Palestine. Jeroboam remained an exile in Egypt until Solomon's death in 922 BC.

Jeroboam was an Ephraimite prince who led a rebellion of the laborers whom Solomon had conscripted from the tribe of Joseph to build the fortress of Millo. His rebellion resulted in the separation of northern Israel, or Samaria, from southern Israel, or Judah.

Jeroboam initially chose Shechem as his political capital. Shechem was a wise choice because of the historical significance it held for Israel. Abraham built an altar at Shechem (Genesis 12:6–7); Jacob's first foothold in Canaan was at Shechem (Genesis 33:18–20); and the tribal confederacy occurred at Shechem (Joshua 24). Also, Jeroboam chose as his sites of cultic worship the cities of

Dan in the north and Bethel in the south. Both of these cities were traditional places of pilgrimage for the Israelites. He placed a shrine of a golden calf in both and established feasts and festivals at these shrines. This gave the northern kingdom a religious foundation that could compete with the dominant influence of the temple of Yahweh in Jerusalem. Once the altars were in place, Jeroboam called the nation to worship, proclaiming, "You have gone up to Jerusalem long enough. Behold your gods, O Israel, who brought you up out of the land of Egypt" (1 Kings 12:28). Therefore, one of Jeroboam's first acts as king was to lead his country into apostasy.

Although Ahijah of Shiloh gave Jeroboam a favorable prophecy before he became king, Jeroboam grew to despise prophets. 1 Kings 13:1–10 tells of a prophet of Judah who traveled all the way to Bethel to inform Jeroboam that his altars would be torn down and turned to ashes. When Jeroboam stretched out to seize the prophet, his arm withered and froze in midair. After Jeroboam apologized, the prophet restored his arm. When Jeroboam invited the prophet home, the prophet replied, "If you give me half your house, I will not go in with you" (1 Kings 13:8).

Later Jeroboam's son, Abijah, fell sick. Jeroboam sent his wife in disguise to the prophet Ahijah of Shiloh. Although Ahijah was blind, he knew of Jeroboam's wife's coming by means of the Lord. He pronounced doom on the whole house of Jeroboam. Not only would every male member of Jeroboam's house be cut off, but they would be eaten by dogs and birds and not be buried in graves (1 Kings 14:9–12). Jeroboam's wife went back to Tirzah, which had recently superceded Shechem as the capital of Israel. When she entered her house, Abijah died. Thus began the fulfillment of Ahijah's prophecies against the house of Jeroboam.

Nadab (910–909 BC) 1 Kings 15:25–32

Nadab was the son of Jeroboam I. He became king during the second year of Asa of Judah and reigned only two years, continuing in the evil path of his father. He was later assassinated by one of the royal officers, named Baasha. With his death, the rule of the house of Jeroboam I came to an end.

Baasha (909–886 BC) 1 Kings 15:33–16:7; 2 Chronicles 16:1–6

Baasha was a ruthless and cruel leader who ruled over Israel for twenty-four years, beginning in the third year of King Asa of Judah. To protect his throne, he ordered the slaughter of the entire house of Jeroboam. The prophet Jehu son of Hanani prophesied that Baasha's house would be destroyed as a result of its violent nature. Although Baasha died a natural death in Tirzah, his descendants reaped the evil he sowed.

Previously, an alliance between Baasha and Ben-Hadad I of Damascus led Baasha to extend his forces to Ramah, located five miles north of Jerusalem. Ben-Hadad I later changed his alliance to Asa of Judah when Asa offered him tribute. This allowed Asa to push his border northward, reclaiming some of the territory that Baasha had taken.

Elah (886–885 BC) 1 Kings 16:8–14

Elah, the son of Baasha, reaped the whirlwind spawned by his father. He took the throne in the twenty-sixth year of the reign of King Asa in Jerusalem and inherited the capital of Tirzah from his father. One night during the second year of his reign, while Elah was drunk and senseless, Zimri, an official in his army, crept into the royal chambers and murdered him, thereby fulfilling Ahijah's prophecy.

Zimri (885 BC) 1 Kings 16:15–20

Zimri's coup d'etat lasted only one week. Like Lee Harvey Oswald, who assassinated President John F. Kennedy only to be gunned down in custody two days later, Zimri's short reign began and ended in violence. It was as if God used Zimri as his instrument to carry out Ahijah's prophecy. Zimri's legacy is that he butchered the house of Baasha, set flames to the royal palace and took his own life: "And when Zimri saw that the city was taken, he went into the citadel of the king's house, and burned the king's house over him with fire, and died" (1 Kings 16:18).

Omri (885–874 BC) 1 Kings 16:21–28

The man who benefited most from Zimri's theft of the throne was Omri. Omri was another commander of the army of Israel.

He opposed Zimri's seizure of the crown from the house of Baasha. Omri led his troops against Tirzah, motivating Zimri's suicide. He gained the throne of Israel in the twenty-seventh year of King Asa of Judah. Omri kept the capital of Israel in Tirzah for six years, and then he officially moved the capital to the city of Samaria where it remained throughout the rest of the history of Israel. This proved a brilliant move, as Samaria was on a sloping hill, which made it easy to defend. Omri restored a measure of stability to Israel. John Bright, author of *A History of Israel*, notes of him:

> Omri was obviously a man of great ability. The Assyrians referred to Israel as "The House of Omri" long after his dynasty had been overthrown. Omri's policy for Israel's recovery was patterned in its major features on that of David and Solomon; it called for internal peace, friendly relations with Judah, close ties with the Phoenicians, and a strong hand east of the Jordan, particularly against the Arameans.[1]

Because of his military power, he was able to quash a rebellion led by Tibni. He had to contend with Ben-Hadad of Damascus, who had already seized territory in Galilee and the Transjordon from Israel. Omri formed an alliance with Phoenicia in the north by having his son Ahab marry the Phoenician king's daughter, Jezebel. Because Syria was a natural enemy of each of these nations, Phoenicia and Israel both gained from this marriage. Omri also faced Ashur-nasirpal II, who was reviving the power of the Assyrian state.

The Moabite stone, discovered at an archaeological dig in Diban in 1868, tells how "Omri, king of Israel, humbled Moab many years." This record goes on to state that Israel controlled Moab for forty years, "during his [Omri's] time, and half the time of his son [Ahab]." This extra-Biblical evidence substantiates the existence of Omri and Ahab.

Although Omri gave Israel a sense of political stability, 1 Kings 16:25 notes his evil legacy, "Omri did what was evil in the sight of the LORD, and did more evil than all who were before him."

Ahab (874–853 BC) 1 Kings 16:29–22:40; 2 Chronicles 18:1–34
Ahab inherited Omri's throne in the thirty-eighth year of King Asa's reign, and he ruled over Israel for twenty-two years. He

---

[1] John Bright, *A History of Israel*, 3rd ed. (Philadelphia: The Westminster Press, 1981) 240.

forged alliances with many of the foreign nations around him in order to stabilize Palestine. Having married Jezebel, the daughter of Ittobaal, king of Tyre, Ahab proceeded to adopt the worship of Baal. He ordered the construction of a temple to Baal in Samaria and offered sacrifices to Baal on the altar of Yahweh.

Ahab also arranged the marriage of his daughter Athaliah to Jehoram the son of Jehosaphat of Judah. This brought security to the country, but it also allowed the contaminating influence of Jezebel's religion to reach down into Judah.

During his reign, Ahab had much to fear. Ben-Hadad I of Damascus was busy attempting to overtake the land of Israel. When Ben-Hadad and Ahab met in battle, the leader of Damascus was taken captive by Ahab. Instead of executing Ben-Hadad for his aggression, Ahab pardoned him and sent him back to Damascus with a treaty from Israel. An unknown prophet severely rebuked Ahab for his light treatment of an enemy of Israel (1 Kings 20:35–43).

However, Ahab had bigger things on his mind than Ben-Hadad. The Assyrians under Shalmaneser III (859–824 BC) were attempting to bring all of western Asia under their control. In 853 Ahab and Ben-Hadad I met Shalmaneser III in a battle at Qarqar on the Orontes River. As recorded on the Black Obelisk of Shalmaneser III, now in the British Museum, Shalmaneser boasts that he "made the blood of his enemies flow down the valleys and their bodies were scattered far and wide." If this statement is true, it remains a mystery why Shalmaneser III withdrew to Assyria without noticeable change to the lives of the citizens of Israel or Damascus.

Later in his reign, Ahab joined forces with Jehosaphat of Judah to take back Ramoth Gilead from the Arameans. The prophet, Micaiah ben Imlah, prophesied disaster for Ahab. Ahab experienced the truth of the prophecy when he fell dead from the wound delivered by a Syrian arrow.

During Ahab's reign, there was considerable material prosperity in Israel. Ahab began many building campaigns and kept a powerful, effective army in the land. In spite of these positive signs, deterioration was also evident. Bright writes:

But there are signs of a progressive disintegration of the structure of Israelite society, and of a harsh system that tended to place the poor at the mercy of the rich. The former, forced in hard times to borrow from the latter at usurious rates of interest, mortgaging their land, if not their own persons or those of their children, in security, faced and, one gathers, not infrequently (2 Kings 4:1) the prospect of eviction, if not slavery.[2]

Spiritually, Ahab followed in the steps of his father, Omri. He was even more evil than his father. "Ahab did more to provoke the LORD, the God of Israel, to anger than all the kings of Israel who were before him" (1 Kings 16:33). It is no wonder that during the reign of this evil king, God decided to send the greatest of his prophets, Elijah.

Ahaziah (853–852 BC) 1 Kings 22:51–2 Kings 2:25

After Ahab's death, his son, Ahaziah, succeeded him to the throne. Only a few months into his reign, Ahaziah suffered a fall that left him incapacitated (2 Kings 1:2). His plight grew worse when he made the unwise decision to seek help from Baal-Zebub, the pagan god of Ekron. "Baal-zebub" means "Lord of the Flies," a mocking taunt used instead of "Baal-zebul," meaning "Lord of the Divine Abode" or "Baal, the Prince." ("Baalzebul" or "Beelzebub" later became a synonym for Satan in Jewish theology.) The prophet Elijah pronounced judgment against Ahaziah for his action.

The Biblical text records that Ahaziah sent three different battalions of fifty soldiers to capture the prophet Elijah. Elijah sat upon a hill waiting for each battalion. As they demanded Elijah's surrender, he called fire to fall upon their heads, and they were destroyed. This happened to two battalions. The third battalion tried a different tactic. Instead of demanding Elijah's surrender, they requested that Elijah surrender himself—he did—demonstrating the respect that should be shown to a prophet of God.

Ahaziah later died and was succeeded to the throne by his brother, Jehoram (or Joram).

Jehoram (Joram) (852–841 BC) 2 Kings 3:1–8:15

Jehoram had the dubious distinction of receiving the crown of Israel from Ahaziah at the same time that Elisha received the

[2] Bright, 244.

prophetic mantle from Elijah. Early in his reign, Jehoram attempted a reform in Israel. This turned out to be "too little, too late," as Queen Jezebel had already done extreme damage. Elisha looked instead to Jehu as the God-appointed leader who would cleanse Israel. Elisha was so certain of this change that he anointed Jehu before Jehoram's death. When Jehoram learned of this, he struck an alliance with Ahaziah of Judah to do battle with Jehu. These forces met at Jezreel. Jehu was victorious and both Jehoram and Ahaziah died in the battle.

Jehu (841–814 BC) 2 Kings 9–10

As Israel's next king, Jehu initiated a bloody purge in the land. He had two objectives: annihilating the house of Omri and the idols of Baal. From Jezreel he ordered the execution of the eighty sons of Ahab in Samaria. His followers sent the eighty heads of Ahab's sons back to Jezreel. He also had forty-two relatives of Ahaziah slaughtered. This action fulfilled Elijah's prophecy against the house of Omri. However, Jehu himself was not interested in fulfilling prophecy, but simply in getting rid of his competition for the throne.

Jehu desired to cleanse Israel of Baalism. Therefore, he lured the worshipers of Baal into the temple and stationed eighty soldiers at the exits. He had the entire assembly slaughtered in cold blood. This massacre rid the land of the foreign god, the Tyrian Baal, and further wiped the land free of the influence of the royal house of Omri.

Jehu associated with Jehonadab, son of Rechab (2 Kings 10:15). Pfeiffer says of Jehonadab:

> He was the first named of a group of Israelites known as Rechabites who sought to maintain the older desert traditions in opposition to the vices of an urbanized society. The Rechabites lived in tents instead of houses and they abstained from the use of intoxicating liquor. As orthodox Yahwists they were sympathetic with Jehu in his efforts to exterminate the last remnants of Baal worship from Israel.[3]

Jehonadab was enthusiastic about Jehu's purge, seeing it as a necessary ingredient for the expulsion of Baal from Israel.

[3] Charles F. Pfeiffer, *Old Testament History* (Grand Rapids, Michigan: Baker Book House, 1973) 317.

But Jehu made a mistake by isolating himself from Judah, Tyre and other neighbors. He left himself open to attack. Hazael (842–806), a servant of Ben-hadad II, had gained control of Damascus by murdering his master in 842 BC. Hazael had hopes of controlling Israel, but he had to wait until Shalmaneser III of Assyria pulled out. In 841 BC Shalmaneser III came marching west from Assyria to control Syria. He also controlled Israel and was receiving tribute from them. Jehu of Israel is depicted on the Black Obelisk of Shalmaneser III as kneeling before the Assyrian monarch paying him homage. Shalmaneser describes himself as:

> ...the mighty king, king of the universe, king without rival, the autocrat, the powerful one of the four regions of the world, who shatters the might of the princes of the whole world, who has smashed all of his foes like pots.[4]

The Assyrian king did not stay in Palestine. Shalmaneser III took his troops back to Assyria leaving Hazael of Damascus an opportunity to control the territory of the Transjordan. Hazael seized Samaria, making Jehu's son, Jehoahaz, a vassal king. Hazael allowed Jehoahaz to employ only ten chariots, fifty horsemen and ten thousand infantry in his military.

Jehoahaz (814–798 BC) 2 Kings 13:1–9

Jehoahaz took the crown of Israel from his father, Jehu, when Israel was at one of her weakest points. Damascus had crippled Israel, making her nothing more than a vassal territory. Her weakness also made her vulnerable to attacks from the Philistines and the Amorites. Because of the limits that Hazael of Damascus had placed upon the Israelite army, Jehoahaz could do nothing to protect Israel during this time.

In 805 BC a new Assyrian king came to power. Adad-nirari III was a capable leader who renewed the attacks on Syria that Shalmaneser III had begun. Adad-nirari III brought the Syrians to their knees and made them no longer a threat to Israel.

Joash or Jehoash (798–782 BC) 2 Kings 13:10–14:22

The son of Jehoahaz is identified by two different names, Joash and Jehoash. Joash ruled when Assyria marched on Damascus, which freed Israel to regain control of her territories.

4 Pfeiffer, 332.

Elisha prophesied about these victories just before his death by asking Joash to strike the ground with arrows. Joash responded by striking the ground three times. Elisha grew angry and said,

> "You should have struck five or six times; then you would have struck down Syria until you had made an end of it, but now you will strike down Syria only three times" (2 Kings 13:19).

Next, Joash aggressively pursued his southern neighbor, Judah. At Beth-shemesh, Joash fought against Amaziah, king of Judah, capturing him and moving into Jerusalem, toppling part of its wall. 2 Kings 14:13–14 notes:

> And Jehoash king of Israel captured Amaziah, king of Judah, the son of Jehoash, son of Ahaziah, at Beth-shemesh, and came to Jerusalem, and broke down the wall of Jerusalem for four hundred cubits, from the Ephraim Gate to the Corner Gate. And he seized all the gold and silver, and all the vessels that were found in the house of the LORD and in the treasuries of the king's house, also hostages, and he returned to Samaria.

At this time Joash could have annexed the whole of Judah, but he decided to return home.

Jeroboam II (782–753 BC) 2 Kings 14:23–29

Jeroboam II enjoyed unprecedented success. He was the greatest king of Jehu's dynasty. He expanded the borders of Israel from Hanath as far as the Sea of Arabah. Bernhard W. Anderson allows us to visualize how vast Jeroboam II's territory was:

> The entrance of Hamath, the northernmost boundary of Solomon's kingdom (1 Kings 8:65), refers to the pass between Mount Lebanon and Mount Hermon, which can be located on a map by drawing a line straight across from Damascus to Sidon. The Sea of the Arabah refers to the Dead Sea, named after the low desert plain that extends from the Jordan valley to the Gulf of Aqabah. Thus Jeroboam II extended his kingdom northward into the orbit of Hamath and Syria, and southward into territory that encroached upon Judah. Never before had an Israelite king held undisputed sway over so large a kingdom.[5]

[5] Bernhard W. Anderson, *Understanding the Old Testament*, 4th ed. (Englewood, Cliffs, New Jersey: Prentice-Hall, 1986) 286.

His territory extended from the Dead Sea in the south to as far north as the kingdom of Israel had stretched in Solomon's reign.

Jeroboam II was supported by a prophet named Jonah ben Amittai who saw him as a savior of Israel. Samaria gained great wealth as a result of Assyrian weakness and of the opening of trade routes closed since Solomon's day. This new material gain was not shared by all. Wealthy landowners and traders greedily kept the less fortunate in poverty. With the newfound wealth, the gods of the surrounding nations were welcomed back into the land, and Baal once again found a home in Israel.

Jeroboam II's reign was marred by corruption and a destruction of the spiritual vitality of Israel. The prophets Amos and Hosea both caustically attacked his hypocritical and heartless rule.

Zechariah (753–752 BC) 2 Kings 15:8–12

Jeroboam II left Israel in a weakened state after his death. In the following two decades, Israel had five kings, three of whom ascended to the throne through violence.

Zechariah's reign began in the thirty-eighth year of Uzziah of Judah and lasted just six months. He continued the evil of his father, Jeroboam. Shallum, the son of Jabesh, murdered Zechariah right in front of a public assembly. This fulfilled the prophecy made to Jehu, "Your sons shall sit upon the throne of Israel to the fourth generation" (2 Kings 15:12).

Shallum (752 BC) 2 Kings 15:13–16

Through violence, Shallum took over the reign of Israel in the thirty-ninth year of Uzziah, king of Judah. Shallum sowed the wind and reaped the whirlwind. As he ascended the throne by assassination, so Menahem, the son of Gadi, assassinated Shallum only one month into his reign.

Menahem (752–742 BC) 2 Kings 15:17–22

After the murder of Shallum, Menahem gained control of Israel in the thirty-ninth year of the reign of Uzziah. He reigned in Samaria for ten years. He continued in the evil of his predecessors. One incident in his reign particularly demonstrates his evil nature—his treatment of Tiphsah (or Tuppuah), a city which refused to open its gates to him. He destroyed this Israelite city and killed its citizens. To fully desecrate the city, he ripped open the wombs of the pregnant women, exposing their unborn children.

As was true of other kings of Israel, Menahem's major opponent was the rising power of the Assyrian state. In 739 BC, Pul of Assyria (also known as Tiglath-Pileser III) marched into Israel, demanding tribute from Menahem. The Israelite king placated Pul by giving him one thousand talents of silver (thirty-seven tons). In order to pay this tribute, he extracted heavy taxes from the people. This, however, did not hurt the wealthy, who simply passed along the cost of the taxes to the poor. From this time on Israel remained a vassal state to the mighty Assyrian Empire.

Pekahiah (742–740 BC) 2 Kings 15:23–26

Pekahiah, the son of Menahem, received his father's crown in the fiftieth year of Uzziah of Judah's reign. He ruled for two years, continuing the evil of his father. Pekahiah was assassinated by fifty Gileadites led by Pekah ben Remaliah, the captain of Pekahiah's military.

Pekah (752–732 BC) 2 Kings 15:27–31

Pekah began his reign in the fifty-second year of Uzziah. He reigned for twenty years in Samaria. He continued the evil of Jeroboam II. Pekah, an officer of Pekahiah, had assassinated the king and gained the throne for himself.

Pekah took Israel down a road of ruin. He joined an anti-Assyrian coalition with Rezin of Damascus in hopes of forcing the Assyrians out of Palestine. To strengthen their coalition Pekah and Rezin looked south to Judah. They hoped to crush Judah and plant a vassal king on Ahaz's throne, thus securing Judah's help against Assyria. To stop this coalition, Ahaz appealed to Tiglath-Pileser of Assyria for help. In 734 BC Assyria swept into Palestine, stopping the threat of the Syria-Israel coalition before continuing on to the border of Egypt.

During his reign, Tiglath-Pileser of Assyria invaded Israel, taking captive Abel Beth-Maacah, Janoah, Kedesh, Hazor, Gilead and Galilee. He also took all the land of Naphtali, deporting her people into captivity. Hoshea, the son of Elah, assassinated Pekah.

Hoshea—The Last King of Israel (732–723 BC) 2 Kings 17:1–6

In 733 BC Tiglath-Pileser attacked Israel. Hoshea ben Elah surrendered to Assyria and paid them tribute to keep Assyria from devastating Samaria. In 732 BC Tiglath-Pileser entered Damascus, sacked the city and killed the Syrian King Rezin, deporting many Syrians back to Assyria.

When Tiglath-Pileser was succeeded by his son, Shalmaneser V, Hosea thought he had an opportunity to throw off the heavy shackle of Assyrian domination. He sought out Pharaoh So of Egypt to form a coalition with the Egyptians against the Assyrians. Shalmaneser V caught wind of this and viewed Hoshea as a traitor. In 724 BC Shalmaneser V attacked Israel and after gaining control of most of the nation, he headed toward the capital city. For two years the Assyrian king laid siege to the city of Samaria. During this time, Shalmaneser V died, and Sargon II took his place. Hoshea was captured in Samaria and placed in prison.

The Deportation and Resettlement of Samaria (721 BC)

The decadent and disastrous history of Israel is summed up in 2 Kings 17. The kingdom of Israel ended in 721 BC when Sargon II concluded Shalmaneser V's campaign, sacking Samaria and taking 27,290 inhabitants of Israel as captives back to Assyria. Sargon II repopulated Israel with foreigners taken captive in other Assyrian victories. 2 Kings 17:24 reads,

> And the king of Assyria brought people from Babylon, Cuthah, Avva, Hamath, and Sepharvaim and placed them in the cities of Samaria instead of the people of Israel; and they took possession of Samaria, and dwelt in its cities.

Sargon confirms this in his own records: "[The cities] I set up again and made more populous than before. People from lands which I had taken I settled there." This was the beginning of Samaria and the Samaritan race, which lived on into the first century. The nation of Israel was to exist no more.

Why did Israel fall? Many accusations are leveled against the people of Israel in 2 Kings 17, but one charge rings the loudest—

apostasy. Since the northern kingdom of Israel gave up on God, God finally gave up on Israel. Israel loved the customs of her neighbors and kings instead of the commands of God (2 Kings 17:7–8). She mimicked the religion of her neighbors by secretly building high places in all her cities and by setting up pillars and Asherim for pagan worship (2 Kings 17:9–10). She carelessly rebelled against the commands of God and set up idols to worship (2 Kings 17:11–12). In spite of the warning of prophets and seers, Israel broke covenant with God and forgot his statutes (2 Kings 17:13–17). Israel fell so far that she gave up her sons and daughters as sacrifices for divination and sorcery to Baal and Asherah, just like the pagan nations did. It is difficult to believe that God's chosen people could offer human sacrifices—especially their own children!—but they did. After this list of charges 2 Kings 17:18 concludes, "Therefore the Lord was very angry with Israel, and removed them out of his sight; none was left but the tribe of Judah only." The death knell sounded for Israel. The epitaph on her tombstone read, "They followed worthless idols and themselves became worthless" (2 Kings 17:15 NIV).

Life Application

1. As you read about the northern kingdom, what stands out to you?
2. Ahab and Jezebel had an "interesting" marriage. What can you learn from their relationship?
3. Powerful lessons can be learned from studying the father-to-son spiritual influences. What do you see about family influences as you read about these rulers? How does it affect generations? What are you doing to inspire the faith of children (your own and/or the children of the kingdom)?
4. Over and over again the predictions of the godly prophets came true. How has this helped your faith in God for your life situations? Do you trust God and his promises?

10

LIFE IN THE SOUTH

The life of the Southern Kingdom of Judah was markedly different from that of her sister kingdom (Israel) in the north. Although Israel is never mentioned as having one good king, Judah had good kings mixed in with bad kings. Israel was more materially prosperous than her southern neighbor, but Judah had the temple of Yahweh in Jerusalem and could claim spiritual prosperity because of that. Judah enjoyed a longer rule than Israel and survived the invasion of Assyria, though she was unable to withstand the forces of the Babylonian empire in the sixth century. We will now survey the kings of the southern kingdom of Judah.

The Southern Kingdom of Judah
Rehoboam (922–913 BC) 1 Kings 11–14; 2 Chronicles 10:1–12:16
Rehoboam was not the wisest administrator to ever take office. When he received the crown from his father, Solomon, he was faced with the greatest crisis in the history of the united confederation—civil war. He traveled from Jerusalem to Shechem in the north in an attempt to hold together the fragile bond of unity between the tribal states.

Rehoboam's one chance for maintaining unity quickly slipped through his fingers when he decided to follow the counsel of his junior advisors instead of his senior advisors (1 Kings 12:6–11). His junior advisors suggested that Rehoboam punish the northern tribes. Rehoboam announced that the hardship faced in the North under Solomon would seem light compared to his heavy hand."My father made your yoke heavy, but I will add to your yoke; my father chastised you with whips, but I will chastise you with scorpions" (2 Kings 12:14). Rehoboam was basically saying,

"They thought my father was tough? Wait till they get a load of me!" He had not learned the fine art of winning friends and influencing people.

The northern half of Israel decided to try their luck with their old slave master, Jeroboam, who was back from exile in Egypt. Rehoboam barely made it back to Jerusalem alive. He had to flee from Shechem on a chariot to Jerusalem, where he gathered forces to wage war against the northern tribes. A prophet named Shemaiah counseled him against this action. The kingdom of Israel was now split in two—Israel/Samaria in the north and Judah in the south.

In Rehoboam's fifth year, Shishak, king of Egypt and founder of the twenty-second Egyptian dynasty, broke the three-hundred-year lull in aggression between his people and Judah by marching into Judah. Shishak stole all the treasure from the temple and from Solomon's royal palace (1 Kings 14:25–26). Solomon's glory quickly faded—because he had failed to train his son.

Abijam or Abijah (913–911 BC) 1 Kings 15:1–8; 2 Chronicles 13:1–22

Abijam's reign is summarized in a few quick words, "His heart was not wholly true to the LORD his God" (1 Kings 15:3). He became king in the eighteenth year of Jeroboam of Israel, and his rule was marked by constant conflict with the inhabitants of the northern kingdom. This conflict centered around one of Israel's cultic shrines, Bethel. Abijam was able to secure the territory in Ephraim around Bethel (2 Chronicles 13:19). This gain was short lived, as the next king of Judah, Asa, had trouble securing his own capital, Jerusalem. As was true of many of the other kings of Judah, Abijam left behind a terrible legacy—he took Judah further away from God.

Asa (911–870 BC) 1 Kings 15:9–24; 2 Chronicles 14–16

Asa brought memories of David back to the hearts of the Judeans; he was the first of Judah's reformers. He became king during the twentieth year of Jeroboam's reign in Israel, and he ruled over Judah for four decades.

Since the dark days of Solomon's decline, Judah had fallen deeply into sin. Asa began a program of reform to revitalize the worship of Yahweh in Jerusalem. He drove out men who were cult prostitutes and cleared away the idols. He refitted the temple with silver and gold from his own resources. His zeal for Yahweh led him to renounce his own mother, Maacah, because she had given herself to idolatry (1 Kings 15:13).

Asa, like Rehoboam, faced aggression from his southern neighbor, Egypt. Zerah, "the Ethiopian," invaded Judah and met the forces of Asa at Marehah. Asa defeated Zerah, chased his troops back to Gerar and brought to a close Egyptian tampering in Judean affairs in his generation.

Asa also sought to fortify his northern border. He went to war against Baasha of Israel. Baasha's army advanced to Ramah, only five miles north of Jerusalem, putting pressure on the capital city and placing all of Judah in a compromising situation (1 Kings 15:16–22). Therefore, Asa drew up an alliance with Ben-Hadad I, the king of Damascus. Ben-Hadad broke his treaty with Baasha to come to the aid of Asa, because his troops were available to the highest bidder. They forced Baasha out of Judah and back to his home territory.

Jehoshaphat (870–848 BC) 1 Kings 22:1–50; 2 Chronicles 17–20

Jehoshaphat reigned for a quarter of a century in relative peace. However, the prophet Jehu ben Hanani rebuked the king for cooperating with King Ahab of Israel. His cooperation went to the point of allowing his son, Jehoram, to marry the daughter of Ahab and Jezebel, Athaliah. This would have disastrous effects in the future as the union allowed Jezebel's influence to reach down from Samaria into Jerusalem.

In an attempt to copy the maritime expeditions of King Solomon, Jehoshaphat wanted to send ships to Ophir in exchange for gold. It is possible that he even used Solomon's ships for this venture. He convinced Ahaziah, king of Israel, to join him as a partner. A prophet, Eliezer ben Dodavahu of Mareshah, warned Jehoshaphat against such an attempt (2 Chronicles 20:37). The ships were destroyed even before they left port.

Jehoshaphat started another revival in Jerusalem. He abolished idolatrous shrines and ordered the priests to go throughout the land, teaching the people of the cities to follow the book of the Lord. He did not, however, go as far as his father, Asa, had gone. He allowed the high places to remain.

Jehoram (848–841 BC) 2 Kings 8:16–24; 2 Chronicles 21

Jehoram married Athaliah, daughter of Ahab and Jezebel, in a move to secure the border between Judah and Israel. It seems he succumbed to Jezebel's influence through her daughter because Jehoram killed all his brothers and partisans in an attempt to secure his throne. This violence did not provide security because Jehoram died very early in his reign of a disease of the bowels (2 Chronicles 21:18–20).

Ahaziah (841 BC) 2 Kings 8:25–29; 2 Chronicles 22:1–9

Ahaziah was the son of Jehoram and Athaliah, the grandson of Ahab and Jezebel. He died in the first year of his reign, a victim of the purge of King Jehu of Israel.

Athaliah (841–835 BC) 2 Kings 11; 2 Chronicles 22:10–23:15

When her son Ahaziah died, Athaliah, the daughter of Ahab and Jezebel, seized the throne of Jerusalem. It is difficult to believe that a granddaughter of the king of Tyre could wear the crown of David, but it happened. She continued in the way of her mother, infecting Judah with the worship of Baal. She attempted to murder all the surviving members of the Davidic line (a move that God had predestined to fail). This slaughter would have included her own children and grandchildren. An infant son of Ahaziah, Joash (Jehoash) was rescued by his aunt, the wife of the priest Jehoiada (2 Chronicles 22:11). Joash was the only one left to carry on the line of David.

Joash or Jehoash (835–796 BC) 2 Kings 12; 2 Chronicles 23–24

At the age of seven, Joash was presented at the temple by the priest Jehoiada to become king. Jehoiada held the power of Joash's throne during his youth. Jehoiada proficiently lead a coup against Athaliah by using the ancient spears and shields of David that were housed in the temple. He also hired a group of mercenaries known as the Carites. When Athaliah ran into the temple, crying treason, she was chased out and executed.

Jehoiada then initiated a reform in Judah. He smashed the idols of Baal that Athaliah had erected. Jehoiada gathered up the priests of Baal and executed them. He ordered a collection to be made to repair the temple in Jerusalem. The new king set up a collection booth by cutting a hole in the top of a chest and setting it by the altar at the entrance of the temple (2 Kings 12:9). Sadly, this reform ended when Joash came of age.

Joash did not share the ideals of his uncle, Jehoiada. When Jehoiada died, Joash again allowed Baalism to flourish in Jerusalem. When Jehoiada's son rebuked the king, Joash responded by having the man, his cousin, killed (2 Chronicles 24:22).

During Joash's reign, Hazael of Damascus began to extend his power. Threatened by this, Joash stripped his own palace and the temple of its treasure to pay as tribute to Hazael. Joash had reason to fear Hazael, for he was the greatest king Damascus had known, skilled both as a warrior and as a builder. He was shortsighted, however, as seen in 802 BC when Adad-nirari III of Assyria (811–784 BC marched into Damascus, making Hazael a vassal of the Assyrian state.

The people of Judah were dissatisfied with the rule of Joash. He was assassinated by his own servant for the good of the people (2 Kings 12:21).

Amaziah (796–767 BC) 2 Kings 14:1–22; 2 Chronicles 2

Amaziah, Joash's son, became the king of Judah in 796 BC. He executed the enemies who had assassinated his father. He also planned an invasion of Edom with soldiers hired from Israel.

When Adad-nirari III (811–783 BC) came to power in Assyria, the pressure which Israel and Judah felt from the throne of Damascus eased. The successors of Adad-nirari III were inefficient leaders, which gave Palestine even more freedom during the next half century.

Amaziah went on to defeat Edom. Then he mistakenly decided to fight Joash of Israel. Joash warned Amaziah of the foolishness of such a venture (2 Kings 14:10–11). These kings locked horns at Beth-Shemesh where Joash captured Amaziah and then marched toward Jerusalem (2 Kings 14:11–14). Joash succeeded in breaking down part of the wall of Jerusalem and taking gold, silver and hostages back to Samaria. Suffering in the popularity polls in Jerusalem, Amaziah fled to Lachish, hoping to lie low until the storm passed. The storm followed him, however, in the form of assassins who took his life.

Azariah or Uzziah (767–740 BC) 2 Kings 15:1–7; 2 Chronicles 26

Like his contemporary in Israel, Jeroboam II, Uzziah enjoyed prosperity due to the short-lived weakness of the Assyrian royalty. He repaired the defense wall surrounding Jerusalem and reorganized the army. Uzziah opened up ports for Judah and extended her borders in the Philistine plain. He expanded Judah's commercial outreach into Arabia and reconstructed her maritime trade through the seaport of Elath. Uzziah developed agriculture during his reign because, as the text reads, "He loved the soil" (2 Chronicles 26:10).

His reign began in the twenty-seventh year of Jeroboam II. He took the throne when he was sixteen years old and ruled for more than five decades, fifty-two years. "He did what was right in the eyes of the LORD, just as his father Amaziah had done" (2 Kings 15:3, NIV). The blemish on his record was his failure to remove the high places in Judah. Later in his life, Yahweh afflicted him with leprosy because of his pride, so that he had to finish his days secluded from the palace (read 2 Chronicles 26:16–19). A limestone inscription in Jerusalem notes, "Hither were brought the bones of Uzziah, King of Judah: not to be opened."[1]

Jotham (740–732 BC) 2 Kings 15:32–38; 2 Chronicles 27

Jotham took over the government of Judah before the death of his father, Uzziah, because of Uzziah's medical condition. He was twenty-five when he began his rule in Jerusalem, which lasted sixteen years. He was able to rebuild the upper gate of the temple of Yahweh. As with his father, Jotham is noted for doing what was right. He too, however, failed to remove the high places from Judah.

---

[1] Charles F. Pfeiffer, *Old Testament History* (Grand Rapids: Baker Book House, 1973) 358.

Ahaz (732–716 BC) 2 Kings 16; 2 Chronicles 28

After the prosperous reigns of Uzziah and Jotham, Ahaz came as a bitter taste to the Judean palate. He received the crown in the seventeenth year of Pekah of Israel at age twenty. He ruled in Jerusalem for sixteen years. 2 Kings 16:3–4 unconditionally condemns the rule of Ahaz,

> He walked in the ways of the kings of Israel and even sacrificed his son in the fire, following the detestable ways of the nations the Lord had driven out before the Israelites. He offered sacrifices and burned incense at the high places, on the hilltops and under every spreading tree (NIV).

Ahaz resembled the kings of the northern kingdom more than the kings of the South.

In 739 BC, Rezin of Aram aligned himself with Pekah of Israel, and together they marched on Jerusalem. They were attempting to force Judah to join them in an anti-Assyrian pact.

They planned to overthrow Ahaz and replace him with their own vassal king. Ahaz was so taken aback by this that he burned his son as a sacrificial offering in the Hinnon Valley to placate the gods and spare Jerusalem. Isaiah counseled Ahaz to forget about the threat of invasion and trust in God. Instead, Ahaz trusted in the power of his military and repelled the Syrian-Israelite army, but not before Rezin recovered Elath for the Edomites.

In retaliation Ahaz sought a treaty with Tiglath-Pileser of Assyria. He entreated him to the point of surrendering his kingdom, saying to him, "I am your servant and vassal." Ahaz took the silver and gold of the temple and the royal treasury and sent it as a gift to the Assyrian noble. Tiglath-Pileser responded by capturing Damascus and executing Rezin in 733–732 BC.

Going against the advice of the prophet Isaiah, Ahaz traveled to Damascus to meet with Tiglath-Pileser. He sketched the pagan altar in Damascus and ordered a replica of it built in the temple of Yahweh in Jerusalem. This altar became the official altar of the Jerusalem cultus. Ahaz wanted to accommodate Assyria and he was willing to sell out his God and the national religion to do so.

Hezekiah (716–687 BC) 2 Kings 18–20; 2 Chronicles 29–32

Hezekiah was as different from his father, Ahaz, as day is from night. Anderson says of him:

> The accession of Hezekiah in 715 BC marked a turning point in Judean affairs. Ahaz had been a weak king, a servile and frightened vassal of Assyria. Hezekiah, however, was a wise and vigorous leader, whose policies brought about a religious reformation and a stiffening of Judah's attitude toward Assyria.[2]

Hezekiah received the crown in the third year of Hosea of Israel when he was twenty-five years old. Hezekiah reigned for twenty-nine years.

> He did what was right in the eyes of the LORD, just as his father David had done. He removed the high places, smashed the sacred stones and cut down the Asherah poles. (2 Kings 18:3–4 NIV)

Hezekiah was able to accomplish what other great kings of Judah were not. He carried his reform from the high places around Judah to the center of the temple in Jerusalem. He smashed the copper serpent, Nehushtan, which had been made by Moses and was venerated as a sacred object for centuries (2 Kings 18:4). Hezekiah was unique. 2 Kings 18:5 notes, "Hezekiah trusted in the LORD, the God of Israel. There was no one like him among all the kings of Judah, either before him or after him" (NIV).

Hezekiah's religious reforms inspired political reforms. The cleansing of the religion led to a desire in the hearts of the Judeans to be free from all outside influences, including Assyrian military control. To stay free of Assyria, Jerusalem needed to strengthen her defenses. Because Jerusalem's fresh water had to be brought from the Spring of Gihon outside the city wall into the Pool of Siloam inside the wall, Jerusalem was vulnerable to siege. (This was learned in the Syro-Israelite crisis under King Joash.) Hezekiah decided to dig a tunnel connecting these two sources of water. This engineering endeavor was called the Siloam tunnel. Anderson describes it as

> ...a tunnel more than 1,700 feet long which was cut through solid rock from the spring to the pool. Workers equipped with

[2] Bernhard W. Anderson, *Understanding the Old Testament*, 4th ed. (Englewood Cliffs, New Jersey: Prentice-Hall, 1986) 341.

wedges, hammers, and picks started boring at both ends simultaneously, and after some winding met in the middle.[3]

This tunnel still exists and is symbolic of Hezekiah's reform in Jerusalem. Besides this great feat, Hezekiah also extended the walls of Jerusalem and refortified her defenses (2 Chronicles 32:5).

It is impossible to separate Hezekiah's reign from the events that shook the Assyrian empire during his lifetime. Much of Hezekiah's policies and decisions were based on the strengths and weaknesses of Assyria. Later in his life, Hezekiah's greatest mistake (apart from not trusting God) was underestimating the strength of the Assyrians.

In 721 BC, Sargon II ruled Assyria. He was greeted by a general rebellion from every corner of his empire. He subdued the rebels first on one front and then on another. The last front to be engaged was Palestine, thus giving the people in that region a temporary degree of security and freedom. In 714, Ashdod rebelled and was quickly quashed by the Assyrian sword. Hezekiah decided to stay out of the fray, hoping for a future opportunity to gain Judah's freedom.

In 704 BC that opportunity arrived when King Sargon died in a battle. It proved to be a serious defeat for the Assyrians. When Sargon's son, Sennacherib, took the throne (704–681 BC), Hezekiah refused to pay tribute to Assyria and made his bid for independence. Hezekiah attempted to rally his neighboring countries to join the rebellion against Assyria. From Sennacherib's own records we learn that when Padi, the king of Ekron, refused Hezekiah's plea, his subjects handed him over to Hezekiah to be held as a prisoner in Jerusalem.

In 701 BC Sennacherib turned his eye toward Judah. He first crushed Tyre, reclaiming Assyrian control there. This was enough of a show of power to force many Palestinian states to surrender to Assyria without a fight. But Ashkelon, Ekron and Judah still held out. First Sennacherib took control of Ashkelon and then moved south to Ekron, which he overran, executing and deporting its citizens. Bright describes what happened next:

[3] Anderson, 342.

Meanwhile he [Sennacherib] turned on Judah. He tells us that he reduced forty-six of Judah's fortified cities and deported their population, while shutting Hezekiah and the remnant of his troops up in Jerusalem—like a bird in a cage. The slaughter must have been fearful (cf. Isaiah 1:4). Excavations at Lachish, which Sennacherib stormed, reveal, along with evidences of destruction, a huge pit into which the remains of some 1,500 bodies had been dumped and covered with pig bones and other debris—presumably the garbage of the Assyrian army.[4]

Hezekiah's desired victory was now hopeless. He tried to appease Sennacherib's anger by stroking his wallet. Hezekiah gave Sennacherib all the silver that was found in the temple and in the royal treasury in an attempt to buy Jerusalem's freedom. Yet Sennacherib sent his supreme commander to the capital city to conquer it. The commander challenged Hezekiah saying no god could now save Jerusalem (2 Chronicles 32:15).

Hezekiah sought out the prophet Isaiah and asked him to petition God to provide an escape from this situation. God's answer came, telling Hezekiah not to worry, that he would provide a way out. During the night God sent an angel into Sennacherib's camp, killing 185,000 men. The Assyrian army returned to Nineveh where Sennacherib was assassinated by his own sons, Adrammelech and Sharezer. His son Esachaddon succeeded him to the Assyrian throne.

At some point in his reign, Hezekiah fell sick to the point of death (2 Kings 20). Isaiah went to visit him and notified Hezekiah that the end had come. Isaiah's words were, "Set your house in order." Hezekiah's reaction and God's response demonstrates how much God blesses people with pure hearts. Hezekiah responded to Isaiah's message by repenting.

> Then Hezekiah turned his face to the wall, and prayed to the Lord, saying, "Remember now, O Lord, I beseech thee, how I have walked before thee in faithfulness and with a whole heart, and have done what is good in thy sight." And Hezekiah wept bitterly. (2 Kings 20:2-3)

[4] John Bright, *A History of Israel*, 3rd ed. (Philadelphia: The Westminster Press, 1981) 286.

Yahweh answered Hezekiah's prayer by adding fifteen years to his life. As a sign of God's promise to Hezekiah, the shadow went back ten steps on Hezekiah's sundial.

Manasseh (687–643 BC) 2 Kings 21:1–18, 2 Chronicles 33:1–20

Once again, a godly king passed his throne to an ungodly son. Hezekiah was praised more than any other king of Judah; Manasseh, his son, was condemned more than any other. Hezekiah failed to train his son, and the entire kingdom suffered for it. The events after Hezekiah's death are noted by Bright:

> Between the death of Hezekiah and the final fall of Jerusalem to the Babylonians there lay precisely a century (687–587). Seldom has a nation experienced so many dramatically sudden reversals of fortune in so relatively short a time. Through the first half of the period she was a vassal of Assyria, Judah then knew in rapid succession periods of independence and of subjection, first to Egypt, then to Babylon, before finally destroying herself in futile rebellion against the latter. So quickly did these phases follow one another that it was possible for one man, as Jeremiah did, to have witnessed them all.[5]

Manasseh was just a boy of twelve when he inherited the crown of Judah from his father, Hezekiah. He ruled in Jerusalem for more than five decades, fifty-five years—longer than any other king of Judah or Israel. He undid all the good that his father had done.

> He did evil...He rebuilt the high places his father Hezekiah destroyed...He built altars in the temple of the LORD...He built altars to all the starry hosts...He sacrificed his own son in the fire, practiced sorcery and divination, and consulted mediums and spiritists. (2 Kings 21:2-6 NIV)

Manasseh led Israel into an apostasy so great that Judah was said to have done more evil than the nations around them.

God would not allow Manasseh's evil to go unchecked. In 2 Kings 21:10 a group identified as "the servants of the prophets" delivered a message from Yahweh to Manasseh. The message was a note of doom. Yahweh said,

[5] Bright, 310.

> "Behold, I am bringing upon Jerusalem and Judah such
> evil that the ears of every one who hears of it will tin-
> gle...and I will wipe Jerusalem as one wipes a dish, wip-
> ing it and turning it upside down" (2 Kings 21:12 -13).

The apostasy of Manasseh and his son, Amon, was the final nail in the coffin of Judah. God would judge his own nation as he had judged the other nations.

Amon (643–641 BC) 2 Kings 21:19–26; 2 Chronicles 33:21–25

Amon was twenty-two when he became king. He ruled for a mere two years. He continued the evil of his father, Manasseh. "He walked in all the ways in which his father walked, and served the idols that his father served, and worshiped them; he forsook the LORD" (2 Kings 21:21–22). He was assassinated by his servants, who were in turn assassinated by the people of Judah.

Josiah (641–609 BC) 2 Kings 22:1–23:29; 2 Chronicles 34–35

Josiah was Judah's greatest reformer. He gained the throne from Amon when he was just a child of eight and ruled over the nation of Judah for thirty-one years. His noble epitaph read, "He did what was right in the eyes of the LORD and walked in all the ways of his father David, not turning aside to the right or the left" (2 Kings 22:2 NIV). When Jerusalem crowned Josiah king, she received a king the likes of which she had not seen since David.

In the eighteenth year of Josiah's reign, he began a project centered upon the repair and reconstruction of the temple. As a result of this endeavor, the "Book of the Law" was found (2 Chronicles 34:14). When Josiah read this book, he tore his robes as a symbol of repentance and sent envoys to the prophetess Huldah. She prophesied disaster to the kingdom because Israel had forgotten the Book of the Law. The prophetess also spoke grace to Josiah because of the king's penitent heart. The nation would die violently, but Josiah would die while the kingdom enjoyed peace.

Josiah assembled all the people to renew the covenant of God. He removed the Baals and Asherah poles from the temple and burned them. He did away with the pagan priest, the shrines on the high places, the male cultic prostitutes, and the places where the women wove tapestries for Asherah. These practices were traced all the way back to the days of Solomon (2 Kings 23:13). Josiah's reforms were the greatest that Judah would ever experience.

Josiah celebrated a Passover in Jerusalem unequalled by any Passover celebration in the history of Israel. He ousted all the mediums and spiritists from the land. He brought to Judah a purity never before seen in the kings of Judah. As one reads through the text, Josiah's righteous zeal is apparent in the way he went about purifying the land. He cleansed the temple, then Jerusalem, then Judah, and then traveled north to tackle Bethel in Samaria. He toppled the altars of Bethel just as "the man of God" from the south had prophesied three hundred years earlier in the days of Jeroboam I (2 Kings 23:15–18).

A distinctive element of Josiah's reform was a renewed emphasis on the Jerusalem temple as the central sanctuary for all of Judah. The local shrines of Yahweh were eliminated at this time (2 Kings 23:8–9). This meant that all the priests of Yahweh would now be active at the temple in Jerusalem, which helped curb foreign influence on Judah's worship.

In the thirty-first year of Josiah's reign, Pharaoh Neco of Egypt marched his troops along the Euphrates River to form an alliance with the Assyrians. At the battle of Megiddo, Josiah faced Neco in an attempt to turn back this alliance, which would have compromised the integrity of Palestine. To the chagrin of Judah, Josiah was killed in the battle of Megiddo.

The great reformer was dead at the young age of thirty-nine. No one knows the heights to which Judah might have climbed if Josiah had lived to see his fiftieth or sixtieth year.

> Neither before nor after Josiah was there a king like him who turned to the LORD as he did—with all his heart and with all his soul and with all his strength, in accordance with all the Law of Moses. (2 Kings 23:25 NIV)

Jehoahaz (609 BC) 2 Kings 23:31–35; 2 Chronicles 36:2–4

Jehoahaz was twenty-three when he was thrust into leadership in Jerusalem by the untimely death of his father, Josiah. He reigned for only three months before Pharaoh Neco put him in chains and carted him off to Egypt where he died. Neco placed another of Josiah's sons, Eliakim, on the throne and gave him a new name, Jehoiakim.

Like the other great reformers of Judah, Josiah had failed to train his son. After all the great initiatives taken by Josiah to renew Jerusalem spiritually, his sons did not imitate him and his work died. "And he [Jehoahaz] did what was evil in the sight of the LORD, according to all that his fathers had done" (2 Kings 23:32). What a tragic illustration of how quickly one's work can fade into oblivion.

Jehoiakim (609–598 BC) 2 Kings 23:36–24:6; 2 Chronicles 36:5–8

Jehoiakim was twenty-five when Pharaoh Neco placed him on Judah's throne as a puppet king of Egypt. He ruled over Jerusalem for eleven years. Sadly, his father's reforms had digressed into tyranny. Bright states:

> Jehoiakim, moreover, was not a worthy successor of his father, but a petty tyrant unfit to rule. His irresponsible disregard of his subjects is illustrated by his action early in his reign when, apparently dissatisfied with his father's palace, he squandered his funds building a new and finer one and, worse, used forced labor to do so (Jeremiah 22:13–19).[6]

In 601 BC Nebuchadnezzar of Babylon moved against Neco of Egypt, and the two engaged in a battle in which both suffered severely. Nebuchadnezzar returned home to Babylon to reorganize his army, and Jehoiakim saw this as a chance to rebel against him. Nebuchadnezzar did not respond to this immediately, but in 598 BC, the Babylonian army moved into Judah. At this same time Jehoiakim died. His eighteen-year-old son, Jehoiachin, succeeded him, and on March 16, 597 BC (three months later), he surrendered Jerusalem to the Babylonians.

Jehoiachin (598–597 BC) 2 Kings 24:8–17, 25:27–30; 2 Chronicles 36:9–10

Jehoiachin was eighteen when he became king of Judah and he ruled for just three months. In some versions of the Bible he is called Jeconiah in 1 Chronicles 3:16 and Coniah in Jeremiah 22:24. Jehoiachin surrendered Jerusalem to Nebuchadnezzar on March 16, 597 BC, according to Babylonian records. Jehoiachin and the

[6] Bright, 325 –326.

royal family were taken in the first of three deportations to live in exile in Babylon. The Babylonians also took the most talented of the Judeans with them. In all, more than ten thousand people were taken into captivity. Nebuchadnezzar made Mattaniah, Jehoiachin's uncle, king in his place. He changed Mattaniah's name to Zedekiah.

In about 560 BC, after Jehoiachin had been in exile some thirty-seven years, Evil-Merodach, the new king of Babylon, freed Jehoiachin from prison. He gave Jehoiachin a seat at his table and a seat of honor among the exiled kings. The Bible allows us to follow the life of Jehoiachin in exile so we may know what happened to the Davidic line. With Jehoiachin still alive in exile, hope for a new, messianic future remained alive.

Zedekiah (597–586 BC) 2 Kings 24:18–25:21; 2 Chronicles 36:11–23

Nebuchadnezzar set up Zedekiah as his puppet king when he was twenty-one years of age, and he reigned for eleven years. In his ninth year of rule he rebelled and Nebuchadnezzar responded by building siege works around the city. The siege lasted a year—until supplies became so scarce in Jerusalem that Zedekiah's army toppled part of the city's wall and ran to the Babylonians, admitting defeat. "They killed the sons of Zedekiah before his eyes. Then they put out his eyes, bound him with bronze shackles and took him to Babylon" (2 Kings 25:7 NIV). Zedekiah remained a prisoner in Babylon for thirty-seven years.

Nebuchadnezzar eventually set fire to Jerusalem. He burned the temple, the royal palace, and every important building in the city. His soldiers then tore down the walls surrounding the city, leaving it without protection. The troops also took another group of prisoners to Babylon to live as exiles.

Gedaliah (586 BC) 2 Kings 25:22–26

Nebuchadnezzar set up Gedaliah as governor of Judah after the destruction of Jerusalem. Many men, including Jeremiah, hoped that Gedaliah would be the Messiah for the Jews after the order of the great King David. Their hopes vanished when a group of Jewish zealots assassinated Gedaliah. After the assassination these renegades fled to Egypt, kidnapping the prophet

Jeremiah and taking him with them. They hoped that Egypt would respond to their desperate action and secure their homeland from the Babylonians. They were sadly mistaken and were forced to live the rest of their lives in exile in Egypt. Jeremiah died in Egypt, an exile, lamenting the fact that he would not be allowed to die in the promised land.

Life Application

1. Rehoboam chose the advice of his junior advisors over the wise counsel of his senior advisors. Because of this, he lost the unity of his people. What type of advice do you seek? Are you eager to follow advice from godly men and women? Have you recently made any decisions that have resulted in disunity? What can you do this week to restore unity?

2. A consistent problem in both the Northern and Southern Kingdoms was their idolatry. How does idol worship occur in our society today? How has it appeared in your life? How does God feel about it?

3. King Josiah was a great reformer. He read the Book of the Law and inspired the people to renew the covenant of God. Do you have holy respect for God's Book? How are you inspiring others to dig deeply into the Bible?

11

EXILE AND RESTORATION

After the exile of Judah into Babylonian captivity, the mind of the people of Judah changed. No longer could they worship in the temple at Jerusalem. No longer could they offer sacrifices for atonement upon the temple altars. The emphasis of their worship had to change. They formed small groups that devoted themselves to prayer. In these groups they concentrated on the reading of the Torah. In this way Judaism not only survived the exile, but also underwent changes that endure to this day—including the rise of the synagogue, the scribe and the rabbi. This was a great time of testing for the children of Israel. In this chapter we will consider just how well they weathered that test.

Israel in Exile—Life in Babylon and Beyond

The period of the exile lasted half a century, from 586 BC to 536 BC. Babylon's power was uncontested during most of those years. Nebuchadnezzar, the ruler of Babylon, was able to concentrate on domestic affairs such as building temples and beautifying his royal gardens. He reigned until 562 BC, when he was succeeded by three rulers of very short reign. The first of these was Amel-Marduk (Biblical Evil-Merodach) who set Jehoiachin free in 561 BC (2 Kings 25:27–30). In 556 BC the last ruler of the Neo-Babylonian Empire, Nabonidus, began his reign. He was a scholar and an archeologist who alienated the Babylonian priesthood from his favor because of a difference of opinion. In his old age he set up residence in Teima in Arabia, and gave his son Belshazzar charge over the affairs of state. Cyrus, who in 553 BC revolted against Astyages and became the king of the united Medes and Persians, finally led the overthrow of Babylon. He conquered Belshazzar in 539 BC.

Much speculation has been given as to the number of Jews who were exiled to Babylon in 597, 586 and 582 BC. The first deportation seems to have included from 8,000 to 10,000 men of the better classes (2 Kings 24:14–16). One scholar estimates the total number of exiles included 12,000 men, together with 36,000 to 48,000 women and children. This left many in the land of Judea to continue to eke out a living on that land.

Pressure from the tribes surrounding Judea forced many other foreign groups onto the land who claimed territory from that which the exiles had vacated. The Edomites pressured the Kenites, Kenizzites, Calebites and Jerachmellites into Judah. The Ammonite king was responsible for the assassination of Gedaliah, a governor of Judea set up by Nebuchadnezzar, through Ishmael. The population in Judea took on a very mixed flavor. Politically, after Gedaliah's assassination, the Babylonians must have established a Babylonian governor to oversee the land. Socially, there must have been great poverty in the land among the common man as a class of the "new rich" came into being. These vultures inherited the power of the dispossessed landowners who now lived in exile. This created a class struggle in which only the fittest survived.

The religious climate in Judah would have been volatile. The Babylonians encouraged worship according to the official Babylonian cult. While he was in exile in Egypt, Jeremiah protested against the cult of the "Queen of Heaven," Ishtar (Jeremiah 44:18-19). Egyptian animal worship was reintroduced into Jerusalem, and at the same time, the old Canaanite worship of Baal was again brought in from Samaria. The worship of Yahweh was not abandoned, but it was combined with the worship of other cults and with practices drawn from alien religions. True Yahweh worshipers protested against this syncretism, continuing to worship at the temple ruins and lamenting the decline of the true worship of Yahweh in the holy city (see Lamentations).

Meanwhile, the exiles in Babylon were recognized as foreigners who were affiliated to the plebeian class of citizens. They were without the privileges of the Babylonian citizen, yet were distinctly higher in status than the slave class. The Jews were primarily agriculturists who made their living working the fields.

During the next century, the Jews made their way into towns and into the commerce of the city. They eventually were able to make a good living for themselves in Babylon. Upon their return to Jerusalem, many of the patriotic Jews were able to contribute very liberally to the restoration of the temple (Ezra 2:68–69). The Babylonian ruler was tolerant to the Jews in exile, allowing them to rebuild their lives in relative freedom.

The Babylonians allowed the Jews to keep their own social structure and their own form of worship while in exile. The Jewish elders visited and consulted Ezekiel (Ezekiel 8:1, 14:1, 20:1). Ezekiel was a married man who lived in his own house at a place called Tel-Abib (Ezekiel 3:15, 24; 12:3; 24:18). The stability of social life is noted in the register of the families that were kept (Ezekiel 13:9). In contrast, when the Assyrians conquered the northern kingdom of Israel, Sargon scattered the 27,290 inhabitants of Samaria across northern Mesopotamia and Media in an attempt to wipe away any trace of Israel. Nebuchadnezzar, however, allowed the Jews in exile to retain their national identity. They were given freedom to continue the moral and spiritual worship of Yahweh in Babylon.

When the Jews first arrived in Babylon, they expected a speedy return to the promised land. Yet as time passed, they knew they must settle into the Babylonian scene. Many blamed Yahweh for the loss of their homes and their resettlement in Babylon. The Jews in exile lost hope. False prophets grew up from among them. Idolatry continued in their worship. They were separated from the temple and felt religiously isolated.

Although some lost hope, others developed the individual relationship with God that was prevalent in the life of Jeremiah. The devout turned their face toward Jerusalem and prayed to God (1 Kings 8:48). Fasting replaced sacrifice (Ezra 8:21). The food laws could be observed (as seen in the life of Daniel and his friends). The ritual observance of the Sabbath and the practice of circumcision became distinctive and characteristic marks of Judaism during the exile.

Although we do not know the exact time when the synagogue appeared in Jewish worship, it is safe to say that its foundations were laid during the days of the exile. The study of Scripture, which was to become the hallmark of synagogue worship, was the reason the religious spirit of Judaism survived the exile. It was probably during this time that the compilation of the Old Testament in its present form was accomplished. In fact, much of Judaism as it was to survive down through the first century AD, came from the time of the Babylonian exile. The exile was a desperate time in Jewish history, but it was also the catalyst for the survival of Judaism as we know it today.

The Return and the Restoration

Cyrus, the king of the Medes and the Persians, gave the exiled Jews freedom to return to their homeland in 538 BC. The traditional account of the return is derived from the narrative of Ezra 1–6. Some 50,000 Jews returned to Jerusalem in one group from Babylon. In the seventh month after their return, they erected the altar at Jerusalem, and in the second year, they laid the foundation of a new temple. However, the jealousy and accusations of the current residents of the land halted the work of the temple. The people who repopulated Judea knew that the temple was the center of the religious and political life of the Jews. They figured that if they could keep the temple from being rebuilt, then they could possibly keep the Jews fragmented enough to hold onto their lands that they had claimed during the exile. So, the work on the temple stopped until the days of Darius in 520 BC.

In 520 BC the prophet Haggai arrived on the scene and encouraged the rebuilding of the temple. Haggai rebuked the people for spending time and money in rebuilding their own houses while the temple lay in ruins. Haggai was able to motivate the people, and Zerubbabel and Joshua, the secular and religious leaders of the land, got behind the rebuilding project. What had not been accomplished in twenty years was then accomplished in two years. The center of the worship of Yahweh once again stood in Jerusalem.

After the temple was completed in 516 BC, about three-quarters of a century passed without any Biblical narrative being recorded. What we historically know of this time is that the Jews of Judea were living as a small and impoverished group of people, in an area not much more than twenty miles each way and poor in soil. The inhabitants of Judea depended chiefly on agriculture as a means of survival. The Jews enjoyed religious freedom under their Persian governor, but they had lost their political independence and were forced to pay tribute. Their own religious and political leaders generally were inept—the prophets were blind watchmen and the rulers were shepherds without understanding. The temple had been rebuilt, but nothing had been done to reestablish the moral and ethical fiber of the community of Jews.

Therefore, Ezra and Nehemiah came into Jerusalem to call the faithful back to Yahweh. When Nehemiah arrived in Jerusalem in 444 BC, he inspected the walls around the city. He began a rebuilding campaign that was completed in just fifty-two days. During this time, the Jewish community seems to have been a rather loose union of groups held together by social or national ties, all living in a relatively small area around the city.

The opposition to the rebuilding of the walls around Jerusalem came from two sources. First, the governor of Samaria, Sanballat, naturally wanted to keep the walls from being rebuilt. He did not want Jerusalem to rise again to power and influence. Sanballat began to ridicule them and later threatened the work with armed attack. Although these threats were never realized, Nehemiah made the effort to arm his laborers. Second, the major difficulty that Nehemiah had to overcome was the huge dichotomy between the rich and the poor. Jerusalem was a city of poverty. The wealthier classes, the minority, foreclosed on the debts of the poor, taking Jewish children as slaves in payment. Nehemiah put a stop to the despicable practices of the wealthy classes.

Ezra led the people in a restoration of the law. He read the Book of the Law to the people and reinstated its principles into Jewish life. The people were moved to tears upon hearing the law—they responded as if it had been totally forgotten.

As a result of the work of Nehemiah and Ezra, Judaism once again became an exclusive community. The role of the priest took on greater significance. The observance of circumcision, the Sabbath and sacrificial worship in the temple became foremost religious duties. Judaism might be stamped out by sheer force, but after the exile in Babylon and the restoration in Jerusalem, it was no longer at risk of being absorbed into other forms of religion. Although it had not lived up to the high ideals of the prophets, Judaism was here to stay.

Life Application

1. How have the prophets inspired you to be different?
2. Rebuilding the temple and the walls of Jerusalem were paramount for the restoration of the Jewish faith. What are some areas of your faith that need rebuilding? What is the opposition you face? How faithful have you been in sticking to your decisions made to get closer to God?
3. Judaism was Jesus' religion. How has studying the history of Judaism helped your understanding of Jesus and his teachings? How can you continue to add to this understanding?

AFTERWORD

I wanna go to another place
Where my life is filled with grace
Where I can lay my burden down
Where I can sing and dance and jump around
I wanna go to another place
To another place
To another place

—G. S. K.

Life is filled with many ups and downs. I find it difficult to
stay motivated spiritually on a consistent basis. At times I sprint,
and at times I crawl. I want to soar like the eagles, but I find
myself crawling on my belly like a reptile. When I am down, I
look for a place of grace where I can experience the love of God. I
eventually find this safe place in the Scriptures. I often end up
going to the prophets of Israel. They faced much tougher times
than I'm facing and like me, they struggled to stay faithful. They
weren't always victorious, but they did walk with God. They
inspire me.

The prophets were God's messengers. They delivered the
word of God to men. They did this through their speech, their
written messages and their lives. They often did it in spite of
strong opposition. For example, Amos found it necessary to
denounce the organized and institutionalized prophetic guilds of
his day. Jeremiah stood up to the king and all his court prophets.
His unfavorable prophecies were looked upon as curses—but he
did stand up. Nathan had to rebuke King David to his face.
Ezekiel pranced around like a madman in order to get the exiles
in Babylon to hear God's message. Hosea married a prostitute.
When she was unfaithful to him, he bought her out of prostitution. The prophets were radical messengers of God.

When I look to the prophets, they force me to think about my
own relationship with God. What am I willing to do for God?

How radical am I willing to be? Will I stand up to those who oppose God? Will I embrace his message and declare it to other people? Could I have been a prophet of Israel? How can I be a prophet today?

This first volume has introduced the literature of the prophets. We have surveyed the historical background of the Old Testament prophets. We have more carefully examined the Charismatic prophets. But this is only the beginning. In the two proposed volumes to follow, we will survey the great written prophets of Israel and Judah.

As we keep the prophets of Israel and Judah before us, they call us to become all the more prophetic as disciples of Jesus today. God has definitively revealed his word to us in the pages of the Bible. But his message requires messengers—bold, committed and radical messengers. We must drink deeply from the spirit of these prophets of the past, so that through us the voice of Yahweh may be clearly heard in our world today.

APPENDIX

What follows is a list of OT prophecies and the passages in which they are fulfilled in the New Testament. ("Quoted" means the NT writer actually quoted from the OT source.)

Prophecies and Fulfillments		
OT Prediction	**Subject**	**NT Fulfillment**
Isaiah 2:2–4	birth of the church	Acts 2:17ff
4:2–6; 11:1, 10	Branch	John 15:1–6; Romans 15:12
6:9–10	blind and deaf	John 12:40; Matthew 13:14–15; Acts 28:26–27 (all quoted); Luke 8:10
7:13–14	virgin/Immanuel	Matthew 1:23
8:14–15	stone of Zion	1 Peter 2:8 (quoted)
8:17–18	Jesus and disciples	Hebrews 2:13
9:1–2	Gentiles	Matthew 4:15–16
9:6–9	Jesus' character	The Gospels
10:22–23	destruction	Romans 9:27–28
11:1–10	Type of rule/reign	The Gospels
13:9–13	Day of destruction	Matthew 24:29; Mark 13:24
25:8–9	eternal life	1 Corinthians 15:54
26:1	salvation	Acts 4:12; 2 Timothy 2:10
26:19	resurrection	Acts 4:2
27:9	new covenant	Romans 11:26
28:11–12	tongues	1 Corinthians 14:21 (quoted)
28:16	stone of Zion	1 Peter 2:6; Romans 9:33 (both quoted)
29:13	hypocrites	Mark 7:6–7 (quoted)
29:14	wisdom destroyed	1 Corinthians 1:19 (quoted)
32:1–2	reign	Luke 1:29–33
35:1–10	redemption	Luke 2:38; Romans 3:24
35:5–6	gives sight to the blind	Matthew 11:5
35:8–10	highway to God	John 14:6
40:1–2	forgiveness/sins	John 1:29

Prophecies and Fulfillments—*continued*		
OT Prediction	**Subject**	**NT Fulfillment**
40:3–5	prepare highway	Matthew 3:3; Mark 1:2; John 1:23
40:6–9	word eternal	1 Peter 1:24–25 (quoted)
40:10–11	God's shepherd	John 10:11
42:1–4	servant	Matthew 12:18–21 (quoted)
42:5–11	covenant/Gentiles	Matthew 26:28; Ephesians 2:11–13
45:23	judgment	Romans 14:11 (quoted)
49:6	light to the Gentiles	Acts 13:47 (quoted)
49:8	day of salvation	2 Corinthians 6:2 (quoted)
49:18	remnant	Romans 14:11
50:1–9	crucifixion	Matthew 26:36ff; Mark 15
51:1–23	salvation	Acts 4:12
52:13–15	suffering servant— appearance was marred	Philippians 2:1–11
53:1-12	suffering servant	Luke 23:26–56; Philippians 2:1–11
53:1	revealed message	John 12:37–38
53:4	carrying infirmities	Matthew 8:17 [healing]
53:9	Jesus' innocence	1 Peter 2:22
54:1	barren woman	Galatians 4:27 (quoted)
54:13	taught by God	John 6:45 (quoted)
55:3	resurrection	Acts 13:34
56:7	house of prayer	Luke 19:46
59:20–21	new covenant	Romans 11:26
60:1–22	light	John 1:6–9; 8:12
61:1–2	Jesus' teaching	Luke 4:18–21 (quoted); Luke 7:22
62:2	new name	Acts 4:12, 11:26; Philippians 2:9–10
64:4	God's plan	1 Corinthians 2:9 (quoted)
65:1	Gentiles	Romans 10:20 (quoted)
66:24	hell	Mark 9:48
Jeremiah 7:11	den of robbers	Matthew 21:13; Mark 11:17; Luke 19:46 (all quoted)

Prophecies and Fulfillments—*continued*		
OT Prediction	**Subject**	**NT Fulfillment**
9:23–24	boast in the Lord	1 Corinthians 1:31; 2 Corinthians 10:17 (both quoted)
23:5–6	branch	John 15:1–6; Romans 15:12
31:15	Rachel weeps	Matthew 2:16–18 (quoted)
31:31–34	new covenant of forgiveness	Hebrews 8:8–12, 10:16–17 (quoted)
32:6–15	30 pieces of silver	Matthew 27:9–10
32:38–41	God's people	2 Corinthians 6:16; Ephesians 2:11–13
33:15	branch	John 15:1–6; Romans 15:12
Ezekiel 47:12	stream	John 4:12
Daniel 2	the coming kingdom	Acts 2
7:13–14	the son of man	Mark 13:26; Revelation 1:13, 14:14
9:24–27	abomination	Matthew 24:15; Mark 13:14
Hosea 1:10	Gentiles	Romans 9:26
2:23	Gentiles	Romans 9:25
6:6	mercy not sacrifice	Matthew 9:13, 12:7 (both quoted)
10:8	day of Yahweh	Luke 23:30 (quoted)
11:1	out of Egypt	Matthew 2:15 (quoted)
13:14	eternal life	1 Corinthians 15:55 (quoted)
Joel 2:28–32	day of Yahweh	Acts 2:16–21 (quoted)
2:32	salvation	Romans 10:13 (quoted)
3:13–14	day of Yahweh	Luke 23:30; Acts 2:16–21
Amos 9:11–12	throne	Acts 15:15–18 (quoted)
Jonah 1:17	three days	Matthew 12:40
Micah 5:2–5	Bethlehem	Matthew 2:6 (quoted)
7:6	family strife	Matthew 10:35–36 (quoted)
Habakkuk 1:5	scoffers	Acts 13:41 (quoted)
2:3–4	living by faith	Romans 1:17; Galatians 3:11 (both quoted)
Zephaniah 3:9	call on the name of Yahweh	Acts 2:21

Prophecies and Fulfillments—*continued*		
OT Prediction	**Subject**	**NT Fulfillment**
Haggai 2:6–9	new house	2 Corinthians 5:1
Zechariah 3:1–9	Joshua/Satan/branch	John 15:1–6; Romans 15:12
6:9–13	crown for branch	John 15:1–6; Romans 15:12
9:9	colt	Matthew 21:4–7; John 12:15 (both quoted)
11:12–13	30 pieces of silver	Matthew 26:15, 27:3–10
12:8	David	Acts 2:25–29
12:10	pierced	John 19:34–37 (quoted)
13:1	fountain	John 4:12
13:7	sheep scattered	Matthew 26:31; Mark 14:27 (both quoted)
Malachi 3:1	John the Baptist	Matthew 11:10; Mark 1:2–3
4:1	day of Yahweh	Acts 2:17
4:5	John the Baptist	Matthew 17:11–13; Luke 1:17 (quoted)

Who Are We?

Discipleship Publications International (DPI) began publishing in 1993. We are a nonprofit Christian publisher affiliated with the International Churches of Christ, committed to publishing and distributing materials that honor God, lift up Jesus Christ and show how his message practically applies to all areas of life. We have a deep conviction that no one changes life like Jesus and that the implementation of his teaching will revolutionize any life, any marriage, any family and any singles household.

Since our beginning we have published more than 100 titles; plus we have produced a number of important, spiritual audio products. More than one million volumes have been printed, and our works have been translated into more than a dozen languages—international is not just a part of our name! Our books are shipped regularly to every inhabited continent.

To see a more detailed description of our works, find us on the World Wide Web at www.dpibooks.org. You can order books by calling 1-888-DPI-BOOK twenty-four hours a day. From outside the US, call 978-670-8840 during Boston-area business hours.

We appreciate the hundreds of comments we have received from readers. We would love to hear from you. Here are other ways to get in touch:

Mail: DPI, 2 Sterling Road, Billerica, Mass. 01862-2595
E-mail: dpibooks@icoc.org

Find Us on the World Wide Web

www.dpibooks.org
1-888-DPI-BOOK

Outside the U.S.,
call 978-670-8840 ext. 227